HOW TO GIVE A GOOD ACADEMIC TALK

SKILLS FOR SCHOLARS

For a full list of titles in the series, go to https://press.princeton.edu/series/skills-for-scholars

How to Give a Good Academic Talk, Sharon Marcus

The College Handbook: How to Arrive, Survive, and Thrive on Campus, Rachel Gable

The 5 Questions for Ethical Decisions: How to Succeed Without Selling Your Soul, David W. Miller with Susan Richardson

The Career Arts: Making the Most of College, Credentials, and Connections, Ben Wildavsky

Close Reading for the Twenty-First Century, Dan Sinykin and Johanna Winant

Make Your Manuscript Work: A Guide to Developmental Editing for Scholarly Writers, Laura Portwood-Stacer

How to Review Scholarly Books: Reading, Writing, Relishing, Steven E. Gump

The Entrepreneurial Scholar: A New Mindset for Success in Academia and Beyond, Ilana M. Horwitz

How to Mentor Anyone in Academia, Maria LaMonaca Wisdom

On the Art and Craft of Doing Science, Kenneth Catania

Academic Writing as if Readers Matter, Leonard Cassuto

Thinking through Writing: A Guide to Becoming a Better Writer and Thinker, John Kaag and Jonathan van Belle

The Pocket Instructor: Writing: 50 Exercises for the College Classroom, Edited by Amanda Irwin Wilkins and Keith Shaw

Stellar English: A Down-to-Earth Guide to Grammar and Style, Frank L. Cioffi

How to Give a Good Academic Talk

SHARON MARCUS

PRINCETON UNIVERSITY PRESS
PRINCETON & OXFORD

Published by Princeton University Press
41 William Street, Princeton, New Jersey 08540
99 Banbury Road, Oxford OX2 6JX

press.princeton.edu

GPSR Authorized Representative: Easy Access System Europe - Mustamäe tee 50, 10621 Tallinn, Estonia, gpsr.requests@easproject.com

ISBN 9780691249308
ISBN (pbk.) 9780691249322
ISBN (epub) 9780691297934
ISBN (PDF) 9780691249315
Library of Congress Control Number: 2026949443

British Library Cataloging-in-Publication Data is available
Editorial: Matt Rohal and Lindsay Van Horn
Production Editorial: Jaden Young
Jacket/Cover Design: Chris Ferrante
Production: Lauren Reese
Publicity: Alyssa Sanford
Copyeditor: Elisabeth A. Graves

This book has been composed in Arno

Printed in the United States of America

10 9 8 7 6 5 4 3 2 1

CONTENTS

HOW TO GIVE A GOOD ACADEMIC TALK

1

Introduction

I'LL START with a confession.

I love many things about being an academic: teaching and doing research, writing and editing, mentoring and advising. I have even been known to find some joy in committee service.

But I don't always love listening to academic talks. The reason is simple: most academic talks aren't designed or delivered to engage the people listening to them. We've all had to sit through talks where professors showed cramped illegible slides, never looked up from their screens or their scripts, delayed making their most important points, talked down to us or sailed way over our heads, exceeded their allotted time, and capped all that off by failing to answer questions clearly and directly. Some talks are amazing, but the greatest talks often seem impossible to replicate for those of us not blessed with unusual talent and charisma.

I'm not the only one to think that the average academic talk could be a lot better. When I told colleagues that I was writing this book, their most common response was this: "Are you going to tell people how to make their talks less bad?"

Yes, I am.

How to Give a Good Academic Talk will not turn you into the next Mary Beard, Carl Sagan, or Cornel West, but any professor or graduate student with solid ideas, evidence, and reasoning who follows this book's advice will be able to give better academic talks.

Giving talks is one of the most important things academics do. On many academic résumés, the section that typically takes up the most space is the one listing "Invited Lectures and Conference Presentations." Over the course of a career, a professor at a research university might deliver anywhere from a dozen to hundreds of talks to other academics. Scholars give academic talks for many reasons: to get feedback on unpublished work from experts and nonexperts inside and outside their disciplines, to build professional networks, to demonstrate their ability to present information and answer questions. But even scholars who enjoy all those aspects of being an academic often dread speaking in public and worry, not without reason, about their ability to present their work effectively. "Would you like to come give a lecture in my department some time?" is an invitation every academic wants to receive, but many have mixed feelings accepting.

Giving talks is also one of the activities for which academics receive the least guidance. Like many aspects of academia, presentation skills form part of a hidden curriculum: something academics are expected to learn by osmosis, without any explicit instruction. I'm very aware of this because as an undergraduate, I was terrified of speaking in class. If I thought of something to say, my heart would start pounding, I'd get butterflies in my stomach, and I'd decide to save my ideas for my essays. When I started graduate school, I realized I had to do something about this, and I did, but in a makeshift, haphazard way. My advisors were dedicated and attentive mentors who gave me detailed comments on my writing. When it came to presentations, however, they had far less advice, and their feedback usually focused on what I said, not how I said it.

Today, many graduate programs offer workshops on how to write conference abstracts, grant proposals, dissertation prospectuses, teaching statements, and cover letters. But it's still quite common for doctoral candidates to receive no formal training in presentation skills. Many graduate students get no feedback on those skills until the last year of their degree, when they start applying for jobs. At that late stage, most departments give students opportunities to do mock interviews and talks. These mock job talks and interviews typically take place only weeks or even days before the real thing, which doesn't leave students much time to act on feedback about what they're doing well and what they could improve.

After landing a job, professors are likely to give many more presentations, but when it comes to refining and improving them, they're mostly on their own. Given this lack of formal training, it's not surprising that brilliant scholars often deliver talks whose format and delivery don't live up to the strength of their ideas and material.

That's where this book comes in. Whether you're a graduate student who has yet to deliver a talk, an early-career scholar interested in improving your presentation skills, a seasoned academic ready to take your talks to the next level, or an advisor looking for resources to recommend to advisees, this book can help.

Here's a preview of what's to come. Because this book addresses scholars in all disciplines, chapter 2 sets the stage by addressing a question that scholars in the sciences, social sciences, and humanities handle quite differently: To script or not to script? Chapter 3 offers concrete tips for the most important challenge of any talk: engaging audience attention. Chapter 4 tackles how to begin and end a talk, and chapter 5 deals with the question-and-answer sessions that follow most academic presentations. Chapter 6 addresses how best to use slides. To give a talk inevitably involves using our bodies, so chapter 7 covers delivery, chapter 8 guides you through rehearsal, and chapter 9 discusses how to dress. Chapter 10 addresses the most effective ways to deliver a talk using videoconferencing platforms such as Zoom.

As this chapter list suggests, giving a talk requires many different skills, and the information presented here can be a lot to absorb and implement. In an ideal world, you'd read this book long before giving the talk that inspired you to pick it up. In that situation, I recommend reading the book through in its entirety and identifying the tips that you think would benefit you most. Once you've done that, decide which tips you're most open to trying out immediately and which you'd rather save for a later date. If you're a first- or second-year graduate student, you can start working on your top priorities when giving presentations in seminars, colloquiums, and working groups. By the time you give your first major conference paper or full-length lecture, you will be more comfortable with, say, projecting your voice or answering questions and can then move on to honing other skills. If you're a seasoned scholar, you can similarly read the book through before starting to develop your next presentation and decide what would be most useful to experiment with in the short and long term.

This book is designed to be useful to speakers at all career stages, so at various points, I flag where expectations tend to be different for early-, mid-, and late-career scholars. I'll note here that it's generally prudent for early-career scholars to err on the side of formality and strict adherence to disciplinary protocols. While in principle academia thrives on innovation and originality, in practice people give established scholars more leeway for winging it or marching to their own drummer.

If you have picked up this book days or weeks before giving a talk, I recommend focusing on chapter 4, which covers effective ways to begin and end talks, and chapter 5, on fielding questions well. Unless you thrive under pressure, now is not the time to redesign your slides or rethink your costume (unless you haven't yet decided what to wear, in which case, take a look at chapter 9).

If you have at least a month between reading this book and delivering your presentation, you have ample time to work with the suggestions in chapter 3, which covers how to engage the audience, and in chapters 8 and 9, on how to rehearse and how to dress.

If you have several months before you give your next talk, consider diving into chapter 7, on training your voice and body for more effective delivery. It's worth a look at any point, but you'll find it easier and more fun to act on this chapter's recommendations if you're not in a rush.

Chapter 10, on giving talks on Zoom or other videoconferencing platforms, covers a lot of ground. If you're reading that chapter soon before delivering your talk, I recommend prioritizing the tips about lighting, background, and arranging your computer, desk, and chair. If you have at least a month, that should be enough time to optimize your equipment, find a setting that minimizes disruptions, create slides suited for a virtual presentation, and practice addressing the camera.

This book draws on experience and wisdom I've gleaned from four decades of attending academic talks and discussing them with colleagues, but I've drawn the bulk of my examples from sixty talks delivered between 2017 and 2024. By design, many of those sixty talks are available on YouTube, so that if you're curious, you can consult some of my examples for yourself. You'll find a list of those talks, with links to those available online, at the end of the book. Talks take many forms, and so do my examples, which include full-length lectures and shorter conference presentations, talks delivered from notes and talks read aloud from fully prepared texts, talks delivered in person only, talks delivered only on Zoom, and talks in hybrid formats.

All my examples are real. Everything I recommend for or against is something I've seen people do. When I describe someone doing something well, I name names, to give credit where credit is due. I've mostly anonymized negative examples, out of courtesy, and because anything I advise against doing is not some idiosyncratic blooper but a common misstep I've witnessed many speakers make.

Because this book aims to be useful to academics in a wide range of fields, my examples are distributed more or less equally among the sciences, social sciences, and humanities. In a modest way, *How to Give a Good Academic Talk* aims to transfer skills across disciplines. Talks in chemistry or economics can teach literature professors how to use charts effectively. History presentations can teach biologists or musicologists how to build suspense into their arguments. Art history lectures can teach everyone about contextualizing and analyzing images. As you read this book, you'll be encountering wisdom gleaned from talks on linked administrative datasets, on Herodotus and higher criticism, and on the C-H functionalization of aliphatic amines, without having to attend them—because I did, with an eye and ear attuned to identifying the best practices underlying them.

Where relevant, I cite scientific studies, many drawn from communications and from cognitive science. Researchers have conducted rigorous, controlled experiments on how best to design slides and on whether vocal volume affects listeners more than vocal pace. The chapters that follow situate those technical findings in a cohesive, step-by-step guide and combine them with advice based on my own judgment. Throughout, I aim to make clear when I'm presenting a fact backed by evidence and when I'm offering my considered opinion. You don't have to agree with all of my opinions to benefit from them. If you find yourself arguing with some of what I say, that's great, because it furthers what I assume is your main goal in reading this book: to become more thoughtful about what makes for a good academic talk.[1]

1. I also recommend the following resources, although some of my advice departs from theirs: Stephen M. Kosslyn, *Clear and to the Point: 8 Psychological Principles for Compelling PowerPoint Presentations* (Oxford: Oxford University Press, 2007); Chris Anderson, *TED Talks: The Official TED Guide to Public Speaking* (Boston: Mariner Books, 2017); Jonathan Schwabish, *Better Presentations: A Guide*

At this point, you may be asking yourself why you should listen to me. It's a fair question, and I have a few answers.

First, *How to Give a Good Academic Talk* taps my decades of experience. I began attending talks in 1982 as an undergraduate, delivered my first conference presentation in 1989, and became a professor in 1993. I have given close to two hundred talks and attended close to a thousand and have helped dozens of students develop presentation skills. As a researcher and teacher, sometimes an award-winning one, I've focused on understanding and explaining what makes some stories and performances more absorbing than others. This book also draws on experiences beyond my own. Throughout, I've added other voices to the mix by quoting from interviews that I conducted with eight colleagues known for giving great talks *and* great advice.

Second, if you're a scientist or a social scientist asking yourself what a humanist could possibly teach someone in your discipline about giving a good talk, rest assured that I worried about that myself. I made sure to run my ideas by colleagues in the sciences and social sciences and to include talks from mathematics, statistics, computer science, chemistry, biology,

---

for Scholars, Researchers, and Wonks (New York: Columbia University Press, 2017); David L. Stern, "How to Give a Talk," https://www.howtogiveatalk.com/; Paul N. Edwards, "How to Give an Academic Talk," https://pne.people.si.umich.edu/PDF/howtotalk.pdf; and Lori Flores and Jocelyn Olcott, "A Few Rules of Thumb About Conference Presentations and Invited Talks," in *The Academic's Handbook*, 4th ed., ed. Lori A. Flores and Jocelyn H. Olcott (Durham, NC: Duke University Press, 2020), 64–66. Susan M. Reinhart's *Giving Academic Presentations*, 2nd ed. (Ann Arbor: University of Michigan Press, 2013), also helpful, is designed for undergraduates and international graduate students giving short classroom presentations.

sociology, economics, and political science in my examples. It's also worth mentioning that I wasn't always a card-carrying humanist. In high school, I was a science geek who worked after school in a university biology lab studying programmed cell death in moths. To this day, one of my proudest achievements is having been named a finalist in the 1982 Westinghouse (now Regeneron) Science Talent Search. You can find a photo of me with my fellow finalists online: I'm on the left, head tilted, hand under chin, apparently very ready for my close-up.[2] In college I started out in Brown University's BA/MD program, which meant that before shifting to comparative literature, I took several science courses and one grueling linear algebra class.

Third, if you're a historian, anthropologist, art historian, musicologist, or film scholar or if you work in area studies or on literatures written in languages other than English, you may be wondering if my experience as a humanities scholar is relevant to yours. It is. My research has always been comparative and multidisciplinary, drawing on social and cultural history, visual culture, and media studies. My work as an administrator has also given me valuable experience outside my specific areas of expertise. As an associate dean, I led a division that included Religious Studies, Philosophy, Art History, and Music. In over a decade of service on my university's promotion and tenure committee, including four years as chair, I read hundreds of academic dossiers in twenty-eight disciplines spanning the sciences, social sciences, and humanities. That

2. See https://www.societyforscience.org/regeneron-sts/science-talent-search-1982/.

administrative experience didn't make me an expert in fields far from my own, but it did familiarize me with the norms governing different disciplines, including the norms around talks.

I'll end this introduction with three things that surprised me as I moved from conceptualizing this book to researching it and writing it.

First, I started out assuming that good talks in the sciences, social sciences, and humanities would be so different that each field would require its own separate chapter. I was wrong. The more talks I listened to, the more it became clear that all good academic talks adhere to a core set of principles and practices. I found that when a talk was good, even if I couldn't follow every point being made about Liouville functions or cancer immunology, I could still understand the *moves* the speaker was making. Those moves were the same across disciplines, and they are the moves I share with you here: think of them as the DNA, the norms, the grammar underlying all good academic talks, whether they are full-length lectures, short conference presentations, or book talks. That said, one of my overarching pieces of advice is to learn and follow the norms specific to your discipline and subfield. When it comes to some of my more specific tips, always consult trusted advisors in your discipline and subfield about protocol in your neck of the woods.

Second, I thought that I would need separate chapters to cover the two most common ways of delivering academic talks: loosely, from notes and outlines, or tightly, from a carefully prepared, printed text. Once again, I found this to be something of a false distinction. As the next chapter explains, whether extemporized or scripted, all good academic talks balance organization and flow.

Third, I would not have predicted that every single one of the scholars I interviewed would, at some point in our conversation, evoke theater and performance. Late in my interview with sociologist Michèle Lamont, she revealed that she did theater in high school and college. Historian Daniel Immerwahr described his brother, a theater director, asking him about the "costume" he would wear to deliver a talk and how it would interact with the color of his "set" (also known as his classroom). Physicist Robert Mawhinney capped a magisterial account of the components of a good science talk with this observation: "Talks are not shows, but a little bit of showmanship is not bad." Unlike the first two surprises, this one didn't change my plans. Instead, it reinforced my initial decision to include chapters on delivery, rehearsal, and dress. Academics don't tend to love being in the limelight, but this book will help even the shyest speaker access their inner thespian.

This book is for every academic or budding academic who will ever have to give a talk—which is pretty much every academic—and for every student assigned a presentation in a seminar or working group. As noted above, I recommend going beyond what you read here by consulting colleagues and mentors who can advise you about best practices within your specific field. But if you're hesitant to talk to other people about some of the bigger challenges you face as a speaker, and prefer to start getting advice by reading a book, you're not alone. It's also the case that great mentors don't always give great talks and that even academics who do give great talks can't always explain exactly how they make them so spellbinding. That is why this book has something to offer everyone, from a seasoned scholar delivering their umpteenth lecture to a beginner who has yet to present their first conference paper. Onward, then, to chapter 2, which lays out some basic principles of giving a good academic talk, whether that talk is scripted or not.

2

To Script or Not to Script?

BECAUSE THIS book is written for people in the sciences, social sciences, and humanities, I'm going to start by addressing one of the most striking differences in how scholars in different disciplines give talks. Should you deliver your talk using only schematic notes and slides as prompts, which is the custom among natural scientists and many social scientists? Or should you write your talk out completely in advance, print it, and then read that script aloud word for word, as most humanities scholars do? (Across all disciplines, some academics put very detailed notes on slides that they simultaneously show and read when delivering their talks. No one should do this, for reasons I explain in chapter 6.)

The first time I heard an economist give a paper, I was a newly hired literature professor attending a French studies conference where most of the presenters were in history, literature, and art history. The economist had been invited because he worked on nineteenth-century France. Here's how he started his talk: "I know that humanists read their papers, but in economics, if I did that, people would think, 'What's the matter with him? Doesn't he know his talk?' Which is why I'm going to be speaking without a script."

The economist was correct: In the humanities, people usually don't give talks; they read papers. When he told a group of literary critics and art historians why he wasn't going to read from a script, he followed one of the cardinal rules of delivering a good talk: know your audience and its expectations. Had he simply launched into speaking from notes alone, with no explanation, the humanists at the conference would have been gossiping for days about the scandalous econ professor who showed up without having prepared. That's exactly what I saw happen about twenty years later, when an accomplished senior humanist who often collaborated with scientists decided to take a page out of their book and deliver a fifteen-minute conference talk from notes alone. Hell hath no fury like a disciplinary convention scorned. The audience, humanists all, didn't care that she did a great job. Nor did they notice that her looser delivery made her remarks more engaging. "Why did she do that?," people carped. "Did she care so little about this event that she thought she could just wing it?"

When delivering an academic talk, it's best to follow the protocols you've been trained in, even when your audience follows different rules. Every humanist expert I interviewed for this book agreed that humanities scholars expect speakers to deliver talks that they have written out fully in advance. Similarly, most of the social scientists and natural scientists I spoke with described their discipline's default convention as speaking from notes or slides or preparing a script to glance at as backup but not read verbatim. Even the variations are prescribed. Historians can, by convention, go either way. Political scientists who do empirical research tend to speak from notes, while political theorists who work on philosophical texts usually read prepared texts. Art historians in Europe adopt a more extemporaneous approach than art historians in the United States. The economist in my anecdote wisely chose to follow the rules of *his* discipline, instead of trying out something he'd never practiced before and might never do again. He handled the fact that his humanist audience had different expectations by succinctly acknowledging them and explaining why he wasn't going to meet them.

I initially assumed that this book would require separate chapters, one for what I thought of as ad-libbers and a separate one for script readers. Indeed, while listening to talks in economics and political science in order to research this book, I thought I might need another chapter on a third type of talk I dubbed the disputation. In a disputation, audience members don't wait for the talk to end to start asking questions. They interrupt speakers early and often to raise objections or ask for clarifications. Speakers have to find a way to communicate their key ideas within their limited allotted time while responding to a constant stream of queries. When giving this type of talk, it's important to state all your key points within the first three minutes and to practice giving very succinct answers that allow you to get back to speaking. The disputation format makes time management more challenging, but it also makes presentations more interesting and dynamic, more of a conversation, as one can see if one watches economist Raj Chetty's webinar on the economic impacts of COVID or neuroscientist Dayu Lin's talk on the neural substrates of aggression.[1]

In the end, I decided those separate chapters were not necessary, because I came to see that all good talks strike a balance between order and ease, structure and play. Every good talk, whether it's fifteen minutes or fifty, has been carefully planned and amply rehearsed (for more on rehearsing, see chapter 8). When I first witnessed that economist deliver a talk from notes, it seemed to me as though he just showed up and started talking. I now understand that he almost certainly did not do that. By the time apparent ad-libbers deliver their talks, they've practiced putting their ideas into words many times over. Their talks only seem spontaneous. In fact, the speakers have left very little to chance. Indeed, I would wager that I have never seen anyone actually ad-lib an academic talk. I only thought I had.

A truly ad-libbed talk would almost certainly be a disaster. Delivering talks from notes alone requires years of practice. Doctoral candidates in some fields get that practice by attending weekly working groups in which academics at all career stages present experiments they are conducting, articles they

1. Raj Chetty, "The Economic Impacts of COVID-19: Real-Time Evidence from Private Sector Data," Bendheim Center for Finance, Princeton University, June 17, 2021, posted June 17, 2020, by @Princeton Economics, YouTube video, 1:19:07, https://www.youtube.com/watch?v=ip5pz7gOSwI; Dayu Lin, "The Neural Substrates for Aggression," Federation of European Neuroscience Societies Hertie Winter School 2018 on Neural Control of Instinctive and Innate Behaviour, Obergurgl, Austria, January 6–12, 2019, posted April 27, 2021, by @FENS, YouTube video, 42:44, https://www.youtube.com/watch?v=fZkHshEIp3s. The latter recording cuts off before Lin fully concludes, but there's still ample material.

are reading, and publications they are cowriting. By the time students in these fields give their first talk, they've had years to practice giving coherent, succinct accounts of their research without a prewritten script.

Just as speakers who rely only on notes and slides need to plan and rehearse to stay on track, speakers who read fully scripted papers need to take special care to write texts that are easy on the ears. Listening works very differently than reading, so **design your script to be heard**. Use short sentences that come to a full stop. Alternate short sentences with *very* short sentences. Varying the rhythm of your speech keeps your audience engaged, and shorter phrasing is more memorable. When philosophy professor Mariana Alessandri advises students who are about to give their very first talks, she soothes their nerves by reminding them that they're just reading. Her advice for more seasoned scholars is the opposite: remember that you're not just reading, you're *presenting* (for more on this, see chapter 7). No matter what your career stage, if you script your talks fully before delivering them, make all your sentences conversational, lively, and clear. As Alessandri put it in our interview: when reading a prepared text, "You've got to make the words pop off the page." It's easiest to do that if the words are already popping *on* the page.

If scripting your talk, remember to signpost more often than you would in a printed article or book chapter. People reading an article or book can flip back a few pages if they need help recalling where they have been and where things are going. People attending a talk in person can't hit rewind if they lose focus—and over the course of any talk, even a ten- or fifteen-minute one, most people will lose focus many, many times. For this reason, a scripted talk written to be heard needs to be more explicit about what it's doing and more redundant about what it's saying than an article written to be read (more on this in chapter 3).

When writing out a talk fully in advance, it can be tempting to insert lots of quotes. I recommend resisting that temptation. **When giving an academic talk, paraphrase is your friend.** In print, typography makes visibly clear where your voice ends and other voices begin. But when you give a talk, as Alessandri put it, "You are the voice." Whenever possible, speak as yourself, using your own words. If your research requires presenting long blocks of text, make sure you're analyzing those long quotes in their entirety. If you aren't, shorten them. (For more on this, see chapter 6.)

When speaking from a fully scripted text, consider breaking away from it periodically. Speaking extemporaneously between stretches of reading aloud creates variety, allows for improved eye contact, and can make you feel and sound more grounded in ways that linger even after you return to reading aloud. In our interviews, English professors Rebecca Walkowitz and Nicholas Dames suggested ad-libbing about once every ten minutes, or roughly every 1,300 words. Transitions can be good moments for ad-libbing: you can look up from your text to say something like, "I've just focused on X, which raises the question of Y, to which I now turn." Ad-libs can pave the way for the question-and-answer session: "I would especially appreciate comments or questions about this next part because. . . ." Quick asides can give listeners a peek into your thinking and research process: "I'm still wondering about the ramifications of this" or "I need to see if I can find more examples of that."

Ad-libs also work well for brief mentions of material you had to cut or to preview future directions your work might take. Dames suggested a formulation like, "I don't have time to discuss this in depth, but here's an idea I have more to say about."

Paradoxical as this sounds, it's best to plan in advance exactly *when* to ad-lib. Insert a prompt in your prepared text that summarizes the topic to be ad-libbed in five words or less. Place that phrase in brackets and bold type, as in "[**mention Poincaré embeddings here**]." That formatting makes it easy for you to see at a glance whether a point is optional. When delivering your talk, check the clock each time you reach a bracketed prompt. If you have less time than you thought you did, skip the ad-lib. Even when you have plenty of time, keep your ad-libs brief: aim for one or two sentences that take up between fifteen and thirty seconds.

The key takeaway from this chapter is that all talks should be both well planned and fluidly delivered. If you deliver your talks using notes and slides as prompts, it's easy to sound relaxed, but you'll need to rehearse thoroughly (see chapter 8) to make sure you stick to your allotted time. If you write your talks out fully in advance, it's easy to time yourself in advance, but you'll need to keep your prose simple and punchy and rehearse thoroughly to make sure you deliver your talk gracefully. Whether speaking from notes or reading a script, design your talks to be heard.

For an example of a scripted talk written so lucidly and delivered with so much ease that it was almost impossible to tell when the speaker was reading aloud and when she was ad-libbing, I recommend watching Jewish studies professor Elisheva Baumgarten's lecture on Jews, Christians, and medieval prayer.[2] It's clear from the video that most of the time Baumgarten is reading aloud from the text she holds in her hand, and it's also clear that sometimes she departs from her text to ad-lib. But she's done such a good job of writing smooth prose that her scripted words sound ad-libbed, and she's such a cogent speaker that her ad-libs sound scripted.

Above all else, a good academic talk prioritizes the listeners. Interesting ideas and persuasive evidence are necessary but not sufficient. To give a good academic talk, you have to know how to engage and hold the audience's attention—which the next chapter explains how to do.

2. Elisheva Baumgarten, "Shared Appeals to Different Gods: Jews, Christians and Medieval Prayer," Helen Diller Distinguished Annual Lecture, Center for Jewish Studies, University of California, Berkeley, February 21, 2023, posted March 11, 2023, by @Berkeley Center for Jewish Studies, YouTube video, 1:19:48, https://www.youtube.com/watch?v=904TwPbA7b0.

3

Engaging Your Audience

HISTORY PROFESSOR Daniel Immerwahr, whom I interviewed for this book, is a dynamo: funny, open, and sharp. He's a terrific teacher and dedicated advisor who has written prizewinning books and published essays in the *New Yorker*.

Immerwahr's default mode is enthusiasm, but here's his take on how most people feel while listening to academic talks: "I'm bored and I'm confused."

With that statement, Immerwahr pungently summed up what makes bad talks bad. They fail to hold the listener's attention ("I'm bored"). And they either go over the listener's head or don't make clear how they're saying something new that matters ("I'm confused").

If even scholars frequently feel bored and confused when listening to academic talks, that may be because academics delivering talks often feel nervous and defensive. Here are some of the words theater professor David Levine used in our interview to describe how most academic speakers seem to be feeling: *uncomfortable, scared, armored, guarded, tense.* Levine's diagnosis was that scholars often structure their talks around the fear of being attacked: "Build the ramparts first because you're terrified of getting shot through." Philosopher Mariana Alessandri made a similar point in our interview when she observed that the typical opening of an academic talk is defensive, as if to say, "I know a lot about this so you better take me seriously."

A good academic talk, however, does not prove the superior intelligence of the speaker. A good academic talk focuses on eliciting the attention of its audience. As Alessandri went on to say, "You want to grab them. You want them there with you."[1]

Fine, you'll say. Of course. But *how* do I do that?

The majority of books about public speaking *outside* an academic setting will tell you that the best way to engage audience attention is to elicit an emotional response that fosters connection. That does indeed work—if you're toasting someone, launching a product, or speaking on the campaign trail. It's not as effective with academics, who prioritize evidence, reasoning, and objectivity.

The best way to engage an *academic* audience's attention is to highlight for listeners how you are teaching them something new that matters. As education scholars Lannie Kanevsky and Tacey Keighley put it, "Learning is the opposite of boredom and learning is the antidote to boredom."[2] Learning is also the

1. Sociologist Kieran Healy's article "Fuck Nuance," which Immerwahr recommended to me during our interview, makes a similar point: a good academic talk should make points that the audience finds interesting, not signal that the speaker is smarter than everyone listening to it. To spark interest, a speaker needs to convey a desire "to substantively engage" with an audience "rather than intellectually subdue it." Kieran Healy, "Fuck Nuance," *Sociological Theory* 35, no. 2 (2017): 124.

2. L. Kanevsky and T. Keighley, "To Produce or Not to Produce? Understanding Boredom and the Honor in Underachievement," *Roeper Review* 26, no. 1 (2003):

opposite of being confused. If you start your talks by explaining to your audience what they'll be learning from your talk and why it's interesting and important, you will immediately get their attention.

Once you get that attention, you have to hold it. Attention is fragile.[3] At any given moment someone in your audience may be momentarily tuning you out to ponder what's for dinner or to remind themselves to cancel their free Hulu trial. As physicist Robert Mawhinney observed during our interview, no matter how knowledgeable the audience, "the act of giving a talk is a human one, and you're dealing with people who may be distracted. As a speaker you have a chance and an obligation to engage them." Good talks constantly reactivate the listeners' attention and compensate for the lapses that will still inevitably occur.

To hold your audience's attention, you need to teach them something interesting and important in ways that are clear, vivid, significant, surprising, and suspenseful.

Okay, sure. But if I said that in an academic talk, people would justifiably roll their eyes, because no one would argue with this. When I told people that I was writing a book on how to give a good academic talk, no one ever asked, "Cool, will

---

20–29, cited in Sandi Mann and Andrew Robinson, "Boredom in the Lecture Theatre: An Investigation into the Contributors, Moderators and Outcomes of Boredom Amongst University Students," *British Educational Research Journal* 35, no. 2 (April 2009): 278.

3. See Benjamin T. Sharpe, Michael Geoffrey Trotter, and Beverley J. Hale, "Sustaining Student Concentration: The Effectiveness of Microbreaks in a Classroom Setting," *Frontiers in Psychology* 16 (2025): 1589411.

there be a chapter on how to make talks more obscure, vague, trivial, predictable, and dull?"

What stumps people is *how* to do this.

What follow are powerful, straightforward principles and techniques for keeping academic audiences engaged. I don't discuss how to open and close your talks, because that's the subject of the next chapter. Nor do I talk specifically about slides here, because slides are the topic of chapter 6.

1. Make Your Ideas Matter

The best way to make your ideas matter is to place them in a larger context that the audience already cares about. **Every talk should, within the first three minutes, explicitly or implicitly answer the questions "So what? And who cares?"**

Some talks inherently connect to pressing real-world concerns: cancer, inflation, climate disasters, infectious diseases, how people make decisions. Even highly academic topics can address issues that interest many people: what we mean by beauty, or truth, or adulthood, or how to understand famous works of art.

If your talk hits people where they live, lean into this. I was already paying attention to neurobiologist Leslie Vosshall's talk about mosquitoes because I'm what she terms a "mosquito magnet." But I'd bet that even the lucky folks who rarely get bitten sat up when she said, "We're interested in this animal because it infects over 400 million people a year, so it's important to figure out how they are doing what they do and how we can stop them." Some people don't respond strongly to numbers, so Vosshall brought her point home one more time: "They're waiting to bite you and infect you with these viruses."[4]

A key context for any scholarly talk is scholarship. If you're giving an academic talk, the "who" in "who cares?" is first and foremost the academics who share your specialized knowledge. How do your findings and ideas matter *to other experts*? What are you teaching those experts that they don't already know? Make this explicit: "This is a big issue if you are thinking about X." So central are "so what and who cares?" questions that it can work well to lead with them, as geneticist Rotem Sorek did early in his talk: "Why care about new immune systems?"[5]

A good academic talk also tells the *non*experts in the room why they should care. Academics do highly specialized research, so other people rarely care as much as we do about our topics. But we can make them care. As Immerwahr observed to me, academics are all about loving things that most people don't even know exist—such as the standardization of screw threads, the subject of an entire chapter in his book *How to Hide an Empire*. Immerwahr contended that extreme nerdiness can be an excellent gambit for getting people's attention: "A thing that you find boring, I will make fascinating.

4. Leslie B. Vosshall, "Bitten: Why Are Some People More Attractive to Mosquitoes than Others?," NIH Director's Wednesday Afternoon Lecture Series, National Institutes of Health, October 26, 2022, posted October 28, 2022, by @NIH VideoCast, YouTube video, 1:00:10, https://www.youtube.com/watch?v=XNUlwMfqClg.

5. Rotem Sorek, "The Immune System of Bacteria: Beyond CRISPR," NIH Director's Wednesday Afternoon Lecture Series, National Institutes of Health, January 25, 2023, posted January 30, 2023, by @NIH VideoCast, YouTube video, 1:03:07, https://www.youtube.com/watch?v=_COeBSfG53g.

As academics, we make the world interesting." One of the best ways to make the world interesting is to show how supposedly boring, trivial things are part of a bigger picture. In the case of screw threads, Immerwahr makes readers care about these small but ubiquitous pieces of hardware by showing how they helped make the United States a world power.

Another way to make your ideas matter is to explain how your research builds on and extends other people's work and to invite other people to build on your work. Biologist Tyler Jacks did this throughout his talk, in exemplary ways. He compared his data on lung cancer with data other experts had collected on different tumor types. He contrasted his research to that of another expert in the audience: "This is not T cell editing, Charlie Swanson, this is T cell dysfunction." I didn't get every nuance of that aside, but I did get that multiple researchers are currently studying how T cells interact with cancer cells. Jacks also helpfully connected his presentation to the other conference presentations: "I'm going to transition to another topic now, related to the one I was just discussing and similar to what the previous speaker told you about, and I appreciate her great intro to this topic." Finally, Jacks invited others to build on existing scholarship: "I want to refer to a published study that describes a tool that might be useful to people in this audience." Jacks made his work matter in two ways: he connected his work to curing cancer, a topic most people care about, and he connected his work to research being done by other experts.[6]

6. Tyler Jacks, "Toward Improved Cancer Vaccines: Lessons from Preclinical Models," Koch Institute Symposium 2023, Koch Institute for Integrative Cancer

Another way to make your findings matter is to **take a position in a debate**. Academics love to argue. We feel most connected when most at odds. To get a scholarly audience's attention, don't just assert your point. Make it part of a lively, ongoing controversy.

Academic handbooks often advise people to start articles, books, and talks with a "they say, I say" statement. I agree, but I'd argue (ahem) that the proper order is often "I say, they say." People prioritize what they hear first, and what matters most is your original, innovative point. That's what people came to hear: the as-yet unpublished idea that can teach the experts in the room something new. Start with a quick "I say," then make your ideas part of a larger scholarly debate by showing how what you say is new and surprising relative to what other authorities have said. "They" will have already done a lot of the work to prove the significance of your topic, so "I say, they say" will also demonstrate why your ideas matter.

One good "I say, they say" move is to contrast your approach to common ways of thinking about your topic. Barbara Henry began her talk on Russian literary underworlds with an "I say" move by showing us a slide of a painting depicting the road to Siberia. The painting rendered that road open, level, and endless, establishing Siberia as hell on earth. Henry's "they say" move reminded her audience that world-famous texts by Virgil and Dante had long depicted hell as deep below the earth. She then presented her thesis: nineteenth-century Russian artists differed from their Western European

---

Research, MIT, June 23, 2023, posted July 12, 2023, by @KochInstituteMIT, YouTube video, 1:04:25, https://www.youtube.com/watch?v=0GMl1G4M-0o.

predecessors by placing the underworld on the same plane as ordinary existence.[7] The debate here was not about which authors got hell right—both versions seemed pretty terrifying—but about how evidence typically overlooked in discussions of a topic could change our ideas about it.

Another way to show how your ideas matter is to situate them within an overview of current scholarship in the relevant subfields. If you're giving a talk about what novels can teach us about the history of land use in California, it's great to open your talk by explaining what your work shares with that of "fellow eco-critics," as Carlos Nugent did at the start of a (successful) job talk. That move placed his work in the broad context of an entire subfield. It performed the intellectual service of synthesizing a large body of interdisciplinary scholarship that many of the literature professors in the audience hadn't encountered before. And *that* set him up to explain what he was adding to the mix that other eco-critics had not, which implicitly involved entering a debate about what the field should be studying and how it should study it.[8]

You can turn "they say" itself into a debate by organizing your overview of previous scholarship into camps defined by

7. Barbara Henry, "Road, River, and Book: The Russian Literary Underworld," Sawchen Lecture Series in Slavic Studies, Department of Central, Eastern, and Northern European Studies, University of British Columbia, and Bicentennial Speaker Series, 2020–21, North American Dostoevsky Society, January 26, 2021, posted March 19, 2021, by @North American Dostoevsky Society, YouTube video, 54:09, https://www.youtube.com/watch?v=utjsnbRq2HM. The painting depicted is Isaak Levitan's *Vladimirka Road*, 1892.

8. Carlos Nugent, "Imagining Land and Latinidad in the Wake of the California Gold Rush," Department of English and Comparative Literature, Columbia University, January 31, 2023.

their disagreements, then identifying where you stand in this debate. Which previous findings do you agree with? Which do you extend, complicate, challenge, overturn? Do these apparently opposed camps share an assumption that you are going to question?

Avoid summing up articles one by one. That sounds a lot like a list, and lists are boring. Instead, organize dozens of books and articles into a few competing schools of thought. Even other specialists will sit up and take notice if your literature review takes this form: "School A has addressed the problem this way, while School B has taken a contrasting approach. Neither school has used the framework I will be testing today." Don't summarize, one by one, how ten different critics linked Charles Dickens's novel *Bleak House* to David Simon's TV series *The Wire*. Instead, say, "To date, critics have had three different ways of connecting *Bleak House* and *The Wire*," then offer a fourth.

Occasionally an academic opens up a topic on which there has been almost no previous scholarship. Breaking new ground makes it easy to show how your ideas are original and surprising. Breaking new ground also makes it even more crucial to explain why your innovative claims matter. What caused other specialists to neglect your topic? Michael Brecht addressed this in his lecture on the neurological bases of kinship by pointing out that systems neuroscience had neglected family bonds because for years neuroscientists focused more on atypical behaviors than on common ones.[9] If

9. Michael Brecht, "Blood Is Thicker than Water," Joint Seminars in Neuroscience Lecture, 2021 Winter Series, Brain Research Institute, University of California,

you're talking about an overlooked example, your audience may wonder if previous academics neglected that little-known example because it doesn't merit attention. Zoë L. Henry had to address this challenge when discussing Jessie Redmon Fauset's *There Is Confusion*, a now very obscure 1924 novel by a relatively obscure author. Henry gave her audience several reasons to care about this example. She cited well-known figures who back in 1924 had reviewed the book for major periodicals. She foregrounded the connections between Fauset's modernist novel and other modernist arts, such as dance. And she speculated that scholars had neglected the novel because they hadn't fully understood it, which underscored the importance of her interpretations.[10] By the time she was done, everyone in the room grasped the value of analyzing a work that few had heard of, let alone read, before attending the talk.

2. Make Your Ideas Surprising

Foreground the novelty of your ideas. Often, when academics feel confused and bored, it's not because they don't understand what the speaker is saying. It's because they don't see how it's news. Tell them. As Alessandri said in our interview, an audience should always leave with "some new idea or a new question or a new way of thinking through a problem."

Los Angeles, January 12, 2021, posted January 12, 2021, by @BRI UCLA, YouTube video, 1:05:39, https://www.youtube.com/watch?v=q4W5WcuJjsA.

10. Zoë L. Henry, "The Kinesthetic Turn: Ruth Page, Jessie Redmon Fauset, and the Machinery of Dance Modernism," Department of English, Columbia University, January 22, 2024.

Explaining what makes your research novel is easy enough if you've discovered the Rosetta Stone or invented the theory of relativity, but usually the novelty is more subtle. Maybe you are using new data, like Muriam Haleh Davis, the first scholar writing about a French economic plan for Algeria to use relevant sources written in Arabic. Maybe you are posing an old question in a new way, like John Ma, who began answering the question "What is a polis?" by questioning whether *a* single idea of the polis ever existed. Maybe, like Alessandri, you are boldly avowing, "I love the self-help industry," something we wouldn't expect a philosopher to say.[11]

People pay attention when you surprise them. Highlight how your findings overturn common expectations. In a talk for the general public on his decades-long study of happiness, psychiatry professor Robert Waldinger explained that "the received wisdom about happiness is true but not the whole truth": people say money can't buy happiness, but his longitudinal study showed that basic economic well-being is in fact

11. Muriam Haleh Davis, "The 'Failures' of Liberal Capitalism and the Racial Regime of Religion in Late Colonial Algeria," Society of Fellows and Heyman Center for the Humanities, Columbia University, March 9, 2023, posted March 24, 2023, by @SOFHeyman, YouTube video, 1:18:09, https://youtube.com/watch?v=64OnyV1h6Oo; John Ma, "Polis: The Greek City-State 800 BC–AD 600," Stanford University, April 14, 2011, posted May 25, 2011, by @Stanford, YouTube video, 1:19:34, https://www.youtube.com/watch?v=IEvv1PvVTA0; Mariana Alessandri, "Seeing Ourselves Through Dark Moods," Talks at Google, June 9, 2023, posted June 9, 2023, by @Talks at Google, YouTube video, 47:11, https://www.youtube.com/watch?v=ib21lMQiwe8.

a necessary (though not sufficient) condition for living a happy life.[12]

When it comes to making your ideas surprising, anthropologist Caitlin Zaloom noted in an email exchange with me that another effective way to make audiences sit up and take notice is to **make the familiar strange**. Present something that everyone takes for granted and explain why it's worth interrogating more closely. Zaloom described doing this when presenting material from her book *Indebted: How Families Make College Work at Any Cost*. She would often begin those talks by noting that people in other countries find the U.S. system of paying for higher education bizarre. When she spoke to audiences in the United States, starting this way underscored that something U.S. families take for granted doesn't necessarily have to be that way. When she spoke to audiences outside the United States, that opening comment showed that she did not assume that her case study is the norm everywhere. Instead, her central example was a surprising anomaly in need of explanation—an explanation she would go on to provide.

12. Robert Waldinger, "The Good Life," Lee Kum Sheung Center for Health and Happiness, T. H. Chan School for Public Health, Harvard University, February 27, 2023, posted February 28, 2023, by @Lee Kum Sheung Center for Health and Happiness, YouTube video, 1:02:27, https://www.youtube.com/watch?v=HUHowWFJNBg; viewed live on Zoom.

3. Create Suspense with Questions and Pauses

Years before I started work on this book, I read about a speaker who began a lecture by asking his audience: "What is the secret to happiness?" (Spoiler alert: the answer was *not* economic well-being.) I no longer remember who the speaker was, or where I read about him, but I do remember the story.

The speaker posed the question, and then he waited. And waited. And waited some more. Once the audience figured out that he wasn't going to immediately answer his own question, they took up the challenge and started trying to answer his question for themselves. When he started speaking again, they were 100 percent focused on what he was going to say next, curious whether his response would match their own.

Here was his answer, delivered after watching his audience think intently about his question for a solid minute: "Happiness is being absorbed." He had just proved that very point by making everyone in the audience experience a state of intense concentration. He did *that* by asking a question that his audience could not instantly answer.

Posing questions can be a powerful way to seize and hold your audience's attention. I don't recommend that you typically wait a full minute before you give your answer. I also counsel against asking rhetorical questions that aren't genuine questions, which can seem disingenuous. Asking questions that most of your audience can easily answer is the opposite of suspenseful. If you're not sure whether the answers to your questions are obvious, try them on colleagues who share some of your expertise and see if they all answer the same way.

Ask questions that people can answer only by listening to your talk. A good question creates a "curiosity gap" that only the speaker can close.[13] If the answer is not immediately obvious, even to other experts, then the question will create suspenseful anticipation, leaving people wanting to know what you're going to say next. David Moreno Mateos did this when he asked, "How can we learn from natural settings in restoring urban areas?"[14] Most people see urban settings as the opposite of natural ones, so this isn't a question we can easily answer on our own, which makes us eager to learn how the speaker will resolve the puzzle he has set.

Because questions cue attention, insert them before key points in your talk. Leslie Vosshall already had my attention when she told me that mosquitoes feed on blood *and* nectar. If that's the case, they could be sipping on juice boxes instead of biting me. Vosshall got me even more interested when she turned that fun fact about mosquitoes' dual food sources into a question: "How do mosquitoes tell nectar and blood apart, especially since both contain glucose?" Notice how the

13. In *The Grant Writing Guide: A Road Map for Scholars* (Princeton, NJ: Princeton University Press, 2023), Betty Lai coins the term "curiosity gap" and defines it as the difference between what we currently know and what we need to know that only the grant writer's research will teach us (46).

14. David Moreno Mateos, "Restoring Ecosystems in a Time of Ongoing Global Change," Harvard Museum of Natural History, Harvard University, March 23, 2022, posted November 15, 2022, by @Harvard Museum of Natural History, YouTube video, 48:59, https://www.youtube.com/watch?v=11IX5MmneI0; accessed live on Zoom.

question explains why it's hard to answer: if blood and nectar share a key component, glucose, then mosquitoes can't easily differentiate blood from nectar through taste alone. Because I couldn't easily answer the question, I cared more about the answer. It turns out that mosquitoes have two tongues, a labium for sugar and a stylet for blood, and the stylet that pierces our skin has neurons specially designed to sense blood.

You can pose your thesis as a question, as Philip Maini did when he asked, in a talk about models, "Is the function of a model to make predictions or to understand processes we cannot observe directly?"[15] Once again, his question explained its own difficulty: Here were two competing and plausible definitions, and he was asking us which one we'd choose. It's a complex question because both options sound plausible. Since I couldn't immediately figure out my answer, I was eager to hear his, which was that models help us understand processes we cannot observe directly by transferring knowledge from one domain to another.

I recommend posing questions early in a presentation, not late. Asking questions at the end of your talk can sound like a quiz; asking them early feels more like an invitation. Effective as a very long pause was for the speaker posing his suspenseful question about the secret to happiness, I recommend answering any questions you pose within a few seconds. To maintain

15. Philip Maini, "Squirrels, Turing and Excitability—Mathematical Modelling in Biology, Ecology and Medicine," Oxford Mathematics Public Lecture, Mathematical Institute, University of Oxford, May 27, 2020, posted May 27, 2020, by @Oxford Mathematics, YouTube video, 1:05:51, https://www.youtube.com/watch?v=H-GnVgLS4pM.

audience focus, avoid stringing multiple questions together in a row.

Another way to create pleasurable suspense is to place one part of your argument on hold and turn to another. This works especially well for biographical, ethnographic, and historical narratives. Immerwahr, in our interview, compared this with the structure of a sitcom with A, B, and C plotlines. You don't do all A, then all B, then all C. Instead, you toggle and braid, which requires you to find the most suspenseful places to break off one story before switching to another.

Telling a story out of order makes listeners sit up and pay attention. If your story is about the past, consider starting in the present. If your story is about the present, try starting in the past. Or take a tip from Homer and start your story about the Trojan War not with the abduction that prompted it or the battle that ended it but, rather, in the middle, with Achilles sulking in his tent. Bathsheba Demuth started her talk on whales and whaling this way: "I'm telling a historical story about the past, but I'm going to begin two years ago."[16] Because she was giving a talk as part of a forum on the environment, Demuth could reasonably anticipate that her audience did not consist primarily of fellow historians intrinsically interested in the past but, rather, of people concerned with environmental issues *now*, so she began with a recent event. By telling us at the outset that she had a historical story to tell,

16. Bathsheba Demuth, "Do Whales Judge Us? Interspecies History and Ethics," Environment Forum, Mahindra Humanities Center, Harvard University, November 6, 2019, posted December 5, 2019, by @Harvard University, YouTube video, 1:51:47, https://www.youtube.com/watch?v=yh_kJA0Naug.

then immediately putting that story on pause, she created suspense. As Immerwahr noted, "Everything becomes more interesting if you have to wait for it."

4. Define Your Terms

Often audience members feel bored and confused because they don't understand what the speaker is talking about. This is avoidable. **Define keywords and specialized terms the first time you use them.**

The best speakers understand the importance of defining their terms even when addressing audiences composed largely of fellow specialists. Harvard economics professor Raj Chetty could have safely assumed that people attending a Princeton University webinar hosted by the Bendheim Center for Finance knew how to define "GDP," or gross domestic product. He defined it anyway, prefacing his breakdown with an "of course" that acknowledged that the experts in the room already knew the four components that constitute the GDP. Even more effectively, Chetty made his breakdown significant by folding it into the real point of his talk: how COVID-19, in the first months of the pandemic, affected each of the GDP's components quite differently.[17]

17. Raj Chetty, "The Economic Impacts of COVID-19: Real-Time Evidence from Private Sector Data," Bendheim Center for Finance, Princeton University, June 17, 2020, posted June 17, 2020, by @Princeton Economics, YouTube video, 1:19:07, https://www.youtube.com/watch?v=ip5pz7gOSwI. Similarly, New York University history professor Abigail Krasner Balbale could have assumed that the roughly forty people who chose to attend her talk "The Wolf King: Ibn Mardanīsh and the Construction of Power in al-Andalus" knew what al-Andalus was. Wisely,

"Define your terms" is obvious advice, but many academic speakers don't follow it. Time and again I've heard speakers neglect to define central terms, fail to spell out acronyms, and decide not to translate foreign phrases.

These aren't rookie mistakes. They're *expert mistakes,* the result of people being so knowledgeable about their topics that they've forgotten that other people don't know what they do. This can be a problem even when everyone in the room is in your discipline. As Robert Mawhinney put it in our interview, "Even in a very narrow area, like my own field of theoretical physics, I can be talking to other theorists, but if they work in a different subfield, they think about gravity all the time, and I think about quarks." In that situation, even other advanced specialists will be glad to have basic terms like *quarks* briefly defined.

When preparing a talk, identify what I call its *comprehension precipices*—the points where if your audience stops grasping what you're saying, their understanding falls off a cliff. (See how I defined "comprehension precipice" as soon as I introduced it?) I loved mathematician Philip Maini's talk on the use of models in science.[18] It was designed for the general public, and Maini was so clear that I could follow most of his points, including his explanation of why zebra bodies have more complicated patterns than zebra tails. (The short

---

she didn't. Instead, she began by quickly reminding us that al-Andalus refers to the era when Muslims ruled the Iberian Peninsula. Abigail Krasner Balbale, "The Wolf King: Ibn Mardanīsh and the Construction of Power in al-Andalus," New York University Abu Dhabi Institute, March 30, 2023, posted March 30, 2023, by @NYUAD Institute, YouTube video, 59:31, https://www.youtube.com/watch?v=Z-TXXiz7ZTk.

18. Maini, "Squirrels, Turing and Excitability."

version: more complex patterns need more space to emerge.) I had to concentrate, but as long as he defined his terms, I stayed with him. Then Maini threw out the term "null client"—or maybe it was "null cline." He didn't spell it. He didn't define it. Down the comprehension precipice I tumbled, and I never managed to clamber back up. To be sure, Maini may have meant the final part of his talk to appeal to people with more mathematical knowledge than I have. So, too, speakers who use terms like "PCA," "sensitive cells," "functionalization," and "additive white Gaussian noise" and never define them may reasonably be assuming that everyone in the room is an expert. Fair enough. Usually, I could follow the logic of the talk without understanding every specific. But even when most of the audience knows a term, everyone in the room benefits from hearing exactly how the speaker is using it. Nonexperts in particular learn much better when speakers define key terms succinctly. Given the low cost of explaining key terms and the high returns of doing so, my advice stands: defining key terms is always worth doing.

One of the talks in my corpus of examples was about phages. The speaker assumed that everyone listening already knew what a phage was. I sort of did, but not really. Here's how that went for me: Okay, sounds like phages are eating something, what are they eating? Hmm, seems like a phage is a virus, but wait, seems like phages also *eat* viruses. . . . So, phages are cannibalistic virus-eating viruses? Oh, no, wait, it sounds like phages are viruses that eat bacteria. Got it. I think. . . . Is that right? (After listening some more) Yeah, seems right, but wait, that means bacteria and viruses are different, and I knew that, but how exactly?

As this transcription of my inner monologue shows, while I was struggling to decipher the speaker's basic terms, I wasn't fully listening to him, so I missed some important points. It's the twenty-first century, and anyone in the audience can look up "phage" on their smartphone. But we know how that goes. Once we open that phone to search for a definition, it's hard to resist peeking at news, emails, texts, or social media. If we tune out for even ten seconds, we risk becoming confused in a whole new way and never getting back on track. And once Confusion takes hold, his pal Boredom is rarely far behind.

If you're giving a talk about pterodactyls, start by defining pterodactyls. A biologist who works on mammals and never had a dinosaur phase as a toddler might not know that pterodactyls are actually not dinosaurs but flying reptiles. If you're giving a talk about Elizabeth Bishop's 1976 poem "One Art," a villanelle, define that poetic form. Most of the literature scholars in the room will have heard of a villanelle. Not all of them will remember that a modern villanelle is a nineteen-line poem consisting of five three-line stanzas (tercets) rhyming *ABA* and one final four-line stanza (quatrain) rhyming *ABAA*, in which, sometimes with small variations, the first and third lines of the opening stanza alternately supply the final line of each tercet and the final two lines of the quatrain.

Some specialized terms have become fairly common, like "sunk cost" in economics and "deconstruction" in philosophy. Those are still worth defining for the undergraduates in the audience who may never have heard them before (there's a first time for everyone). It's also the case that once terms become common, people start using them inaccurately and inconsistently, so some audience members may be working with a definition less precise or more idiosyncratic than yours. An added benefit of rigorously defining all key terms: doing so ensures that you truly understand the fancy language you're using (I'm looking at you, "dialectical").

For those worried about taking up too much time with definitions—don't. It takes exactly eight seconds to explain that a phage is a virus that lives inside bacterial cells and infects them. I know, because I timed it. And I spoke slowly. While you're at it, now that you've said that, take another twelve seconds to remind everyone in the room that viruses require a host to survive, while bacteria can thrive inside or outside a host. And then bring it all home: phages are viruses whose host is a bacterium.

It's reasonable to worry that many in the room will feel you're talking down to them if you define simple terms like *virus* and *bacteria*. To offset that concern, explain why you're doing this. Environmental studies professor J. Mijin Cha did that very effectively during her talk on decarbonization by saying, "I know that most of you probably know this, but just so we get some grounding. . . ."[19] Historian Muriam Haleh Davis

19. J. Mijin Cha, "Just Transition or Just a Transition?: The Importance of Power, Organizing, and Framing in Decarbonization," Society of Fellows and Heyman Center for the Humanities, Columbia University, April 25, 2023, posted April 27, 2023, by @SOFHeyman, YouTube video, 1:06:49, https://www.youtube.com/watch?v=bO1KlU0ovJQ. Should you find yourself mainly addressing nonspecialists, make explicit that your talk is not designed for the experts who may also be in attendance. Jaimie Baron handled this elegantly in a presentation about the filmmaker Shirley Clark. The audience included people who'd never heard of Clark and people who knew Clark intimately. Baron said early on, "I know I am speaking to two distinct audiences today—those who know nothing about Clark and those who know more about Clark than I ever will." She then continued, "I

did the same when she prefaced a point with "Just to offer a bit of historical background for nonspecialists."[20] You can make an analogous move just before your talk becomes more complex: "The next section is primarily for the experts in the audience."

Note that I'm not telling you to *avoid* jargon, the technical terminology used by specialists. I'm telling you to *define* it. When speakers use insider lingo and explain what it means, audiences feel included and edified. Jargon words provide useful shorthand—if everyone understands them.

Finally, take care to define disciplinary "terms of art" that assign a specialized meaning to everyday words, like "set" in mathematics. Historian Brodwyn Fischer did a great job of this in a talk on labor in a nineteenth-century port town. Early on, she described herself as working on "what scholars call informality." We've all heard of informality, but colloquially it means something like wearing jeans to the opera. Here's how Fischer headed her audience away from a potential comprehension precipice: "What, you may ask, is informality? Informality is a way of doing things that happens *outside* the restrictions and protections of state law and state institutions."[21]

---

will mainly be addressing those who don't know anything about her." Jaimie Baron, "Countering Culture: Shirley Clarke and the Edges of Cinema," Radcliffe Institute for Advanced Study at Harvard University, March 29, 2023, posted April 6, 2023, by @Harvard Radcliffe Institute, YouTube video, 59:19, https://www.youtube.com/watch?v=YUqEnb6HkUE.

20. Davis, "'Failures' of Liberal Capitalism and the Racial Regime of Religion in Late Colonial Algeria."

21. Brodwyn Fischer, "Intimate Inequalities," Radcliffe Institute for Advanced Study at Harvard University, September 26, 2022, posted March 31, 2023, by

That's a definition even other scholars of informality might appreciate hearing—not because they don't know what informality is but because the speaker just shared a handy way to explain this term of art to undergrads or to colleagues who study formal institutions like courts and parliaments. When you give a talk, you're not just teaching people about your topic; you're also teaching them how to teach it to others.

5. Use the Familiar to Explain the Unfamiliar

The clearest, most vivid way to define unfamiliar terms is to build on what people already know.[22] Sociologist Alison Pugh did this in her talk on "connective labor," a term of art that she defined as paid work that involves empathetically listening to other people.[23] She began with an instance of connective labor familiar to her academic audience: advising students. Next, she listed forms of connective labor that her academic audience members were likely to have heard of but not to have experienced directly: life coaches, personal trainers. Only after those more familiar examples did she turn to her core topic, less familiar when she gave her talk than it is now: attempts to

---

@Harvard Radcliffe Institute, YouTube video, 59:51, https://www.youtube.com/watch?v=0TGMm6LASrU.

22. For more on the science of this, see Susan A. Ambrose, Michael W. Bridges, Michele DiPietro, Marsha C. Lovett, and Marie K. Norman, *How Learning Works: Seven Research-Based Principles for Smart Teaching* (San Francisco: John Wiley & Sons, 2010), 16.

23. Allison Pugh, "The Stratification of Human Contact: The Present and Future of Connective Labour," 2022/2023 Distinguished Speaker Series, Department of Sociology, University of British Columbia, September 6, 2022, https://sociology.ubc.ca/news/watch-dr-allison-pughs-distinguished-speaker-lecture/.

automate connective labor, as when an artificial intelligence chatbot discharges a patient from the hospital.

If you want to explain excitable systems, I don't recommend starting, as Philip Maini did, with obscure examples such as slime molds or complicated mathematical equations. Instead, start with the kind of deeply familiar example he presented later in his talk: the flushable toilet. Everyone can picture the steps involved in flushing a toilet. That makes flushable toilets perfect for explaining the components of an excitable system, which requires a signal (the handle) to breach a threshold that triggers a change (the flush) before returning to a steady state (nonmoving water in the bowl and tank).

6. Provide a Road Map and Engage in Frequent Signposting

Road maps and signposting make a talk's structure and movements clear.

Road maps compactly summarize your talk's key questions, claims, evidence, and methods and enumerate its sections or parts.[24] Road maps work best at the start of a talk, so I discuss them in the next chapter on beginnings and endings.

24. For examples of excellent road maps, see Pugh, "Stratification of Human Contact"; and Elisheva Baumgarten, "Shared Appeals to Different Gods: Jews, Christians and Medieval Prayer," Helen Diller Distinguished Annual Lecture, Center for Jewish Studies, University of California, Berkeley, February 21, 2023, posted March 11, 2023, by @Berkeley Center for Jewish Studies, YouTube video, 1:19:48, https://www.youtube.com/watch?v=904TwPbA7b0. As you will see in chapter 6, I don't think it's necessary to put your road map on a slide, but if you do, both of

Once a talk is underway, signposting tells the audience where you are on the road map.

Signposts occur throughout a talk. They might announce an upcoming landmark or turning point: "Here I arrive at a very important issue" or "Now I'm going to transition to my second question." Signposting can also signal when you are about to slow down, speed up, or bring the journey to a close: "This next point is one I'll go through relatively quickly" or "Here is my last point before wrapping up." Keep your listener moving along a clearly marked and well-described path and they're unlikely to feel confused, because they'll understand where you are going and why.

Some people find signposting cumbersome or superfluous. If you don't like it, don't do it. But I'm a fan. Giving a talk is different from writing an article. What feels redundant in an article is often necessary in a talk to help your audience follow your reasoning and retain your main points. Signposting doesn't just keep listeners on track and provide clarity by explaining what you're doing as you do it. It injects variety by

---

these lectures offer great examples of how to design a road map slide and use it effectively throughout the talk. Two additional examples of good road maps: Jane Ohlmeyer, "Ireland, Empire, and the Early Modern World," Trinity College Dublin and Society of Fellows and Heyman Center for the Humanities, Columbia University, April 21, 2022, posted May 17, 2022, by @SOFHeyman, YouTube video, 1:03:24, https://www.youtube.com/watch?v=Q_a4q03po_k; and Ethan Katz, "The Mothers, the Mamzers, and the Rabbis: Reconstructing Family and Community in Post-Holocaust Jewish Law," Center for the Study of Religion, University of California, Los Angeles, May 8, 2023, posted May 9, 2023, by @Berkeley Center for Jewish Studies, YouTube video, 1:09:05, https://www.youtube.com/watch?v=iht5WIA9vSU.

momentarily zooming out to break the fourth wall. Variety grabs people's attention; clarity holds it.

Moments to signpost include key findings; the significance and originality of specific claims; the details of your reasoning process; transitions; and changes in timing, pace, or level of detail. Below are handy phrases for making those moves.

Phrases to Signpost Key Findings

- "I will emphasize three issues"
- "In this talk, I will"
- "I will be testing two equally plausible hypotheses"
- "When I began, I was interested in how people defined X, but then I shifted to asking why they find X so important"
- "I'm going to tell two different stories about my topic, one about A and one about B"
- "Behind each of these stories lies a question, and that question is"

Phrases to Signpost Significance

If an idea or example is especially important, say so. People's minds wander frequently, so get everyone back in the room with you by announcing when you're about to make a crucial point. Keep in mind that when addressing academics, it's not enough to assert that something matters. They'll want you to explain why.

- "This next point is very important because"
- "What we learn from this is"

- "X has a lot to teach us about Y"
- "What interests us most about X is"
- "As important as X was Y, because"
- "I want you to remember X because it's going to become important later when I talk about Y"
- "Coming back to the theme of X, what it does, and whether it's important"
- "This changes how we think about X by"

Phrases to Signpost Originality

- "There are many surprises in this story"
- "The surprise from this data was"
- "Here's how my questions/findings/methods depart from previous studies"
- "I've told you all this, and now you might think that X should happen. But what if I told you that what happened was actually Y? What would explain that?"

Phrases to Signpost Reasoning Processes

- "How did this come to be?"
- "How are these two apparently unrelated things related?"
- "What can X tell us about Y?"
- "I want to take a minute to point out where we don't need to go"
- "Just for completeness"
- "You might be asking yourself, What about X or Y?"
- "You are probably thinking X and that is true, but"

Phrases to Signpost Transitions

- "I'd now like to turn to"
- "This led us to think that"
- "Some general principles emerging from these studies are"
- "But X changed when Y"

Phrases to Signpost Changes in Timing, Pace, and Level of Detail

- "I'm going to zoom out now to provide some context"
- "This next example is important, so I'm going to spend about ten minutes discussing it in depth"
- "I'm going to have do X fairly quickly"
- "This brings me to the final section of my talk"
- "And this is my final point"

7. Use Examples

A good academic talk uses effective examples. That won't be news to anyone reading this book. Every talk I've ever heard used examples. Some speakers, however, choose and present examples more effectively than others. Some use too many examples; some, too few. Some have great examples but don't introduce them at the best moment. Others fail to explain what point an example makes or how the example makes it.

To understand when to introduce examples and how many to use, let's back up and remind ourselves why talks use examples at all.

First, examples are evidence. People cite examples to prove claims and elaborate on them. Examples can make even outlandish pronouncements seem more plausible. In her famous essay "Mr. Bennett and Mrs. Brown," Virginia Woolf asserted, "On or about December 1910, human character changed." If she hadn't immediately followed that with specific references to Samuel Butler, Bernard Shaw, "the character of one's cook," the story of Agamemnon, and the Victorian couple Thomas and Jane Carlyle, her essay would probably now be forgotten instead of having close to 1,500 citations in Google Scholar and many more across the entire Web.

Second, examples make generalizations more persuasive. If you are a hospital administrator giving a talk on a bioethics panel about how to help nurses get through the COVID-19 health care crisis, it's great to offer a general precept based on experience, such as, "We used humor in our emails." That point would have been even more effective if illustrated with an example of exactly how a specific email used humor, especially because people might wonder what kind of humor is safe for work.[25]

Third, examples make concepts clear by making them easier to visualize. When sociologist Giselinde Kuipers wanted to show that beauty standards have risen over the last 150 years, she used teeth to make the abstract notion of "beauty standards" more vivid, via a slide that memorably contrasted the

25. Leigh Anne McMahon, "Promising Approaches to Moral Distress Among Nurses," panel, Bioethics Program and School of Nursing, Columbia University, June 30, 2022, posted June 30, 2022, by @Columbia SPS, YouTube video, 1:30:39, https://www.youtube.com/watch?v=w-0A9qpej1c&t=2s.

crooked, stained teeth of an ordinary nineteenth-century person to today's straightened, whitened choppers.[26] Computer scientist Moshe Vardi illustrated his claim that resiliency matters more for survival than efficiency by showing a slide that compared cross sections of genetically modified pine with natural pine (Figure 1). The genetically modified pine grew faster and more efficiently, which meant that it had relatively few rings. The natural pine grew more slowly, which meant it had many more tightly packed layers. Which tree, Vardi asked, would be more likely to weather a storm? We could see that the denser trunk would hold up better to strong winds, which concretely reinforced the proposition that fast growth does not necessarily promote survival.[27]

How many examples should a talk use? There's no set rule, but one mistake academic speakers make is to introduce too many. What counts as too many depends on context. A good rule of thumb for a short ten- to twenty-minute conference paper is to discuss only one example in detail. You can mention others, but you only have time to analyze one in depth. For longer talks, a good rule of thumb is **no more than three examples**. After that, people start to find the speaker's point less convincing, not more. So, if you're talking about excitable systems, no more than three. If you're talking about ideal

26. Giselinde Kuipers, "Beauty as Taste and Duty: Value and Privilege in the 21st-Century Beauty Regime," Culture and Social Analysis Workshop, Department of Sociology, Harvard University, October 10, 2023.

27. Moshe Y. Vardi, "Efficiency, Resilience, and Artificial Intelligence," Computer Science/Discrete Mathematics Seminar, Institute for Advanced Study, March 24, 2025, posted March 24, 2025, by @Institute for Advanced Study, YouTube video, 1:13:57, https://www.youtube.com/watch?v=Ji84f7eLxpU.

FIGURE 1. Slide from a talk by Moshe Y. Vardi, "Efficiency, Resilience, and Artificial Intelligence," March 24, 2025. Image used with the permission of Moshe Y. Vardi and the Institute for Advanced Study, School of Mathematics.

tumor antigens, no more than three. Ancient Greek pirate novels, no more than three. Presidential scandals, no more than three. You get it. In fact, you probably got it before I mentioned presidential scandals. That fourth example probably annoyed you. I rest my case.

Scholars can find it challenging to limit the number of examples we discuss. Before developing a claim, we amass heaps of data. It can be hard to resist presenting all of it. Hold back. Choose your two or three best examples, then mention that you have others you'd be happy to discuss during the question-and-answer session (see chapter 5 for more on this). Even claims that go against received wisdom can be effectively proved with a small number of examples discussed in depth. Historian Elisheva Baumgarten's talk on Jews, Christians, and medieval prayer is a good instance of this. Baumgarten persuasively countered the commonly held idea that medieval Jews and Christians operated in isolation from each other by closely analyzing two—and only two—medieval Jewish prayers that incorporated elements of Christian ritual.

Whenever possible, avoid inducing the data stupor that results when people reel off long lists of names, numbers, and facts. Use tables, charts, or graphs to compress large amounts of data into a single image. Natural and social scientists do this all the time, and humanists could learn from them. It's hard for people to take in what you're saying if you recite the number of people emigrating over a given time period from one country to ten others location by location by location by location by location by location by location by location by location. (I know, because I was in the audience when a speaker did this.) Instead, create a chart that enables the audience to compare at a glance the population figures for all ten sites.

There's an art to **placing and explaining examples**. It can be effective to start with a brief example (see chapter 4). I also recommend identifying all of the talk's key examples within the first three minutes of your talk, as part of your road map. Don't analyze them yet; simply mention them without any elaboration at all.

Because examples are evidence supporting a claim, once you're past your introduction, whenever an example appears, the claim it proves should be nearby. Similarly, don't let too much time elapse before you illustrate a generalization with an example. In my opinion, whether the general point precedes the specific example or the example precedes the generalization isn't important. Some people learn best when they have concrete specifics to hold onto; others do better when they start with the abstract takeaway. Cater to both learning styles by toggling between the specific and the general, the general and the specific.

Signpost when you're about to shift from the general to the particular with this simple phrase: "For example. . . ." Signal a shift from specific to general by being equally explicit, as in "What does this case show more generally?"

Don't just articulate what points an example makes; explain *how* it makes them. Even good talks sometimes fail to do this. For example, microbiologist Gagandeep Kang, in a talk about access to vaccines, offered several examples of India developing and manufacturing its own COVID vaccines.[28] Kang did not, however, spell out how vaccine manufacture related to vaccine access, the stated topic. The connection isn't difficult to infer (domestic products are usually more accessible than imports), but it would have been helpful to briefly articulate the link.

Be prepared to go into detail about each of your examples. This includes why you chose these cases and not others. Did you pick an example because it was familiar? Representative? An interesting outlier? Academics are critical thinkers, so they'll be asking themselves whether you've cherry-picked the data to make it prove your point or chosen examples that don't

28. Gagandeep Kang, "Access to Vaccines Without and with a Pandemic: Lessons from India," Mailman School of Public Health, Columbia University, April 19, 2023, posted April 19, 2023, by @Columbia Public Health, YouTube video, 1:26:35, https://www.youtube.com/watch?v=c_e5ockYkOU.

carry enough weight. Anticipate and address those objections, as political theorist Sophie Smith did when she justified her close attention to a now very obscure work of sixteenth-century political theory by mentioning that its author, John Case, was later read by one of the most important political theorists of all time, Thomas Hobbes.[29]

8. Use Tags, Sound Bites, and Metaphors

Tags can help audience members keep track of key people, places, and ideas. Say you're focusing on a famous father and son. Good luck getting nonspecialists to remember the difference between Thomas Arnold and Matthew Arnold when you refer to them by name alone. Instead, show a picture of Thomas, briefly describe him, and tag him as "Thomas Arnold, father, bold educational reformer." Do the same with Matthew, then tag him as "Matthew Arnold, son, melancholy poet." Repeat those tags the next few times you mention each Arnold, and people will start to internalize the differences between Thomas and Matthew.

The brief, catchy sentences we call *sound bites* can also put some pep in your talk's step. One great sound bite in my corpus came in Joseph Koerner's art history talk "Dürer's Mobility." Discussing Dürer's penchant for creating prints made on paper, innovative at the time, Koerner noted that the portability

29. Sophie Smith, "The Nature of Politics," Quentin Skinner Lecture and Symposium, Centre for Research in the Arts, Social Sciences and Humanities, Cambridge University, June 9, 2017, posted June 15, 2017, by @CRASSH Cambridge, YouTube video, 1:04:09, https://www.youtube.com/watch?v=si9iG-093aY.

of that medium turned "images *of* motion into images *in* motion."[30] Shifting to an unusually short sentence grabs audience attention, as nursing professor Rosanne Raso grabbed mine when she summed up what hospital administrators learned from the COVID-19 epidemic: "It's not the worker we need to fix, it's the workplace."[31] Zing! And because short statements are easier to remember than long ones, sound bites also have the added benefit of sticking in people's memories.

Some academics find sound bites reductive, but I think that dismissal is itself reductive. It takes skill to capture a complicated discussion in one compact phrase. Geography professor David Moreno Mateos did that in a talk on climate change when he pronounced that "what takes hours or weeks to destroy may take thousands of years to recover."[32] So did philosopher Mariana Alessandri in a book talk that summed up her analyses of Plato, Aristotle, Seneca, and Epicurus—erudite, heady stuff—as helping readers "feel better about feeling bad."[33]

Because academics value nuance, evidence, and reasoning, I think it's best to introduce a sound bite late in your talk, after thoroughly explaining how you reached your conclusions.

30. Joseph Koerner, "Dürer's Mobility," 2021 Linbury Lecture, National Gallery, January 14, 2022, posted March 7, 2022, by @The National Gallery, YouTube video, 1:34:52, https://www.youtube.com/watch?v=FqsCni1i9AY.

31. Rosanne Raso, "Promising Approaches to Moral Distress Among Nurses," panel, Bioethics Program and School of Nursing, Columbia University, June 30, 2022, posted June 30, 2022, by @Columbia SPS, YouTube video, 1:30:39, https://www.youtube.com/watch?v=w-0A9qpej1c&t=2s.

32. Mateos, "Restoring Ecosystems in a Time of Ongoing Global Change."

33. Alessandri, "Seeing Ourselves Through Dark Moods."

Skeptical, argumentative scholars will believe you when you say, "It's not the worker we need to fix, it's the workplace," if they hear that *after* you've defined exactly what you mean by workers and workplace, presented data to prove your point, talked through that data's limitations, explored alternative ways to interpret it, and provided counterarguments for those who contend that it *is* workers who need fixing.

Like sound bites, *metaphors* can be risky when making academic arguments. As figures of speech that find similarity in difference ("all the world's a stage"), metaphors make connections that can sometimes feel like too much of a leap. On the plus side, metaphors can surprise the listener into paying attention to a phrase whose vividness makes it memorable. Metaphors and similes can also make abstractions more concrete, as when mathematician Tamar Ziegler compared a function's randomness with a drunkard stumbling and reeling as they try to walk a straight line.[34] A good metaphor should hold up when tested. Here again I'll offer an example from Alessandri's book talk, which argued that dolor, or pain, is a sixth sense that, like other senses, can produce knowledge. The metaphor Alessandri developed for pain as perception was "night vision," which equates dark nights of the soul with enhanced powers of sight. "Night vision" is such a resonant formulation because it's simultaneously a concept, a sound bite, *and* a metaphor. Aptly, Alessandri made "night vision" the title

34. Tamar Ziegler, "Sign Patterns of the Möbius Function," Mathematics, Physics & Computer Science Series, Masaryk University, Brno, October 10, 2024, posted March 13, 2025, by @Muni Seminar Series, YouTube video, 55:35, https://www.youtube.com/watch?v=krTUFq8-z-U.

of her book on "seeing ourselves through dark moods"—a subtitle that defines her metaphorical title phrase in colloquial, familiar terms.

9. Repeat Important Points

When talking to a live audience, repetition is your friend. Because people's attention wanders, your message will be clearest when you make it redundant. If something is important, say it more than once. This is a key difference between print and speech.

If you show a graph, reinforce what the x- and y-axes represent the first few times you mention them. If your charts use colors or patterns, label them legibly, and repeat what the yellow dots or pink stripes stand for several times before you start referring to "yellow dots" and "pink stripes" as though everyone listening knows what those represent. If you are talking about the distinction between an explicandum and an explicatum, be aware that most people will have trouble remembering the difference between two such similar words (I know I did, and I took Latin in college).[35] Consider putting the definitions of important or unfamiliar terms on a slide, handout, or whiteboard that people can consult throughout the talk (see chapter 6, on slides).

35. Catherine Herfeld, "Thick Concepts in Economics," Conceptual Engineering Online Seminar Series, June 7, 2022, posted June 15, 2022, by @Conceptual Engineering, YouTube video, 1:08:28, https://www.youtube.com/watch?v=UyJD8xeoIDs.

10. Use Personal Stories (Sparingly)

Here's a final technique for engaging audiences, but one that academic speakers should use in very small doses. In our interview, English professor Nicholas Dames warned against making too many references to the place where one is speaking, and I agree. But people are interested in people, so a brief personal allusion can make speakers and their ideas feel more vivid and significant. Classics professor John Ma modeled this in a talk on the ancient Greek polis, delivered at Stanford back in 2011, when Ma was a professor at Oxford. Early in his talk, Ma gracefully acknowledged the foundational contributions that Stanford classics faculty had made to his lecture topic, simply by saying: "It's an honor to speak here, and a very daunting honor."[36]

Briefly characterizing yourself can help connect you to the audience by humanizing you as a speaker. Introducing her talk on *Night Vision,* Alessandri cracked this dry joke: "What I love about talking about this book is that I don't have to smile."[37] By briefly getting personal, she got my attention, while her downbeat comment wittily performed her book's main point. Fischer prefaced her talk with this graceful (and suspenseful) bit of autobiography: "What kind of historian am I? If this were a game of free association, I'd answer with a string of words: archives, disruptions, stories."[38] That provided a context for the talk that followed and made me curious about how her talk would pick up on each of those terms.

36. Ma, "Polis."
37. Alessandri, "Seeing Ourselves Through Dark Moods."
38. Fischer, "Intimate Inequalities."

I would caution against getting personal by saying, "Let me tell you a little bit about myself as a scholar." Some people can pull this off, but it risks sounding self-important—especially because most speakers who say this proceed to tell us way more than anyone wants to know. We came to hear about the speaker's topic, not about where they went to graduate school, what jobs they've held, or how many important people they know.

A better way to get personal about your scholarly approach is to tell a story about your research process. History professor Bathsheba Demuth did this in her talk on the history of whaling when she said, "Here I'm going to collapse months of work in the coldest archive ever into one paragraph."[39] Mentioning the extreme cold set the scene; I immediately pictured her in a Siberian bunker, wearing a hat and fingerless gloves as she took notes. "Here I'm going to collapse" compactly signposted both a shift in pace and an openness to saying more later, during the question-and-answer session. Tucking her "months of work" into a sentence that was itself doing a lot of other work tactfully evoked Demuth's scholarly qualifications without belaboring them or making them the main point.

In some situations, such as job talks, it can be effective to mention grants that "generously supported" the research being presented; indeed, some grants require this, though you never need to explain that you're thanking a funding agency because you have to. Even when it's not necessary, mentioning grant support can be a deft way to combine an accomplishment with an acknowledgment. Toward the end of your intro-

39. Demuth, "Do Whales Judge Us?"

ductory remarks, you can say something like, "The research I'm presenting today was generously supported by a National Endowment for the Humanities summer fellowship." If funding helped with a specific element of your talk, you can mention it when most relevant, as in, "I'm grateful to the Harry Ransom Center for awarding me a fellowship to consult the archival materials I'm about to discuss." Another way to get personal: connect your talk to one of your publications. "I wrote about this in a recent piece for [journal title]" nests an accomplishment inside a literature review. Limit yourself to one or two such moves per talk. Too much self-citation risks tipping into braggadocio or self-parody.

While writing this book, I listened to a wide range of talks. Some were highly technical and tackled obscure topics I know nothing about, like Ethan Katz's talk on post–World War II Halakhic legal commentary on *mamzerim*, children technically defined as illegitimate. Some were in areas where I have expertise, such as nineteenth-century British intellectual history. Some were user-friendly, designed for even nonspecialists to follow, like Philip Maini's talk on mathematical models. Some were way beyond my grasp, like Tamar Ziegler's talk on Möbius functions. Some covered topics I care about (mosquitoes, cancer, happiness); others addressed subjects I don't find inherently interesting (I'll take the Fifth here). I created this mix deliberately, to ensure that content was not the only factor driving my attention levels. I learned that even when speakers addressed subjects that fascinate me, my attention wavered when they didn't use the techniques outlined in this chapter. Conversely, even when I didn't feel passionate about a topic or understand a talk's every detail and claim, speakers who made the moves described in this chapter kept me engaged throughout.

I began with something Daniel Immerwahr said in our interview and I'll end by quoting him again: "A lecture is you talking to people, and if you're not holding their attention, that's a problem." As an academic speaker, you hold people's attention when you

1. Make your ideas matter within the first three minutes of your talk
2. Make your ideas surprising
3. Create suspense with questions and pauses
4. Define your terms
5. Use the familiar to explain the unfamiliar
6. Provide a road map and engage in frequent signposting
7. Use examples, but no more than three per point
8. Use tags, sound bites, and metaphors
9. Repeat important points
10. Use personal stories, but sparingly

With that in mind, let's turn to two of the most consequential moments of any talk: its opening and its conclusion.

4

Beginnings and Endings

THIS CHAPTER is short and sweet—just as the beginning and ending of a good academic talk should be.

Titles

A talk begins with its title. You have leeway here, but I think that the best titles inform your potential audience about your talk's topic, the methods and evidence/examples you'll use to address it, and the scope of what you'll cover. It's common for academic talks to have titles and subtitles. If you go that route, it can be effective for the title and subtitle to use different registers: make one more colloquial and concrete, the other more erudite and abstract. Since it's always good to start by whetting your audience's curiosity, it can be effective to embed a question into your title or subtitle. Bathsheba Demuth, for example, gave her talk a title that uses simple language to pose a counterintuitive question: "Do Whales Judge Us?" Her subtitle uses more polysyllabic language to evoke the academic fields and topics the talk engaged: "Interspecies History and Ethics."

Leslie Vosshall combined a lurid one-word title, "Bitten," with a straightforward question: "Why Are Some People More Attractive to Mosquitoes than Others?" Titles don't have to be especially clever or vivid, but it's a plus if they are clear. Tyler Jacks's talk is a good example of an effective, plainspoken title: "Toward Improved Cancer Vaccines: Lessons from Preclinical Models." The part before the colon tells us the goal of the research being presented. The part after the colon tells us about the type of evidence being used. It also provides information about the talk's scale, since "lessons" implies an overview rather than a granular account of a single experiment or finding.

Introductions

Academic talks don't begin with the speaker. They begin with someone from the host institution giving an introduction. If it falls to you to introduce someone or if your host asks you to send information to include in their introduction, here are some guidelines.

- When you introduce a speaker, unless you're certain that every single person in the room already knows this, begin by telling people who *you*, the introducer, are.
- Memorize at least the first and last lines of your introduction so that you can deliver them while looking your audience in the eye. There's no reason to be looking down at a piece of paper when announcing that you are very excited to welcome Professor X from University Y. This is especially important if you are introducing the speaker on a videoconferencing platform.

- Name the speaker's most important publications. Speakers give talks in order to test-drive new work *and* to increase people's awareness of the work they've already done. It's also common to mention major fellowships and awards the speaker has won and significant leadership roles they've held, though you can omit those if the speaker has told you they'd prefer a very brief introduction. Always leave out minor details like workshops organized and book reviews published, even if the speaker included those in the bio they sent you.
- Your introduction can do real intellectual work by naming the speaker's hallmarks as a scholar. You might say, "Among Professor X's many important contributions are" or "To give you a sense of Professor Y as a scholar." Identify the broader field in which the speaker works ("Professor Brecht works on the biological basis of play and fun") and say one thing about how their work is helping or has helped to shape that field ("he takes a comparative approach that uses different species depending on the question he's interested in").[1]
- Begin by referring to the speaker using their academic title and last name, even if you are dear friends.
- Keep your introduction short, three minutes or less. You are not the main event, and time is limited.

1. Stephanie White, University of California, Los Angeles, introducing Michael Brecht, "Blood Is Thicker than Water," Joint Seminars in Neuroscience Lecture, 2021 Winter Series, Brain Research Institute, University of California, Los Angeles, January 12, 2021, posted January 12, 2021, by @BRI UCLA, YouTube video, 1:05:39, https://www.youtube.com/watch?v=q4W5WcuJjsA.

- Don't upstage the speaker by being too dazzlingly witty, talking excessively about yourself, or summarizing the talk they're about to give, even if they sent you an abstract.

One of the best introductions in my corpus was the one to Muriam Haleh Davis's talk on Algerian economic history.[2] The introducer didn't introduce himself, so I can't credit him by name, but in every other respect, he gave a model intro. He began by citing Davis's recently published book and explained that it was impacting Middle East studies by correcting a tendency to neglect North African countries. He then recounted first meeting Davis in person at a conference where they were the only two people watching Morocco play in the World Cup. That day, as he put it, two important things happened: Morocco won, and he convinced Davis to come give the talk she was about to deliver. Introductions don't require anecdotes, but this one worked because mentioning that Davis was one of only two people watching a North African team play in the World Cup reinforced the introducer's point about her distinctive expertise in an overlooked field. When the introducer ended by evoking the invitation Davis had accepted in the past, he elegantly mirrored the transition about to take place in the present, from himself as host to Davis as speaker.

2. Introduction to Muriam Haleh Davis, "The 'Failures' of Liberal Capitalism and the Racial Regime of Religion in Late Colonial Algeria," Society of Fellows and Heyman Center for the Humanities, Columbia University, March 9, 2023, posted March 24, 2023, by @SOFHeyman, YouTube video, 1:18:09, https://youtube.com/watch?v=64OnyV1h6Oo.

Preambles

Your talk begins with an actual pre-amble, when you rise from your chair and walk to the front of the room. Don't rush. Take the stage, as Patrick C. Friman advises, with "purpose, poise, and dignity."[3] Turn slowly to face the audience. Make eye contact with a few people. Adjust the podium microphone, if you need to. Smile, if you care to. Pause slightly, and then begin to speak.

We're all at least a little nervous when we face the public, especially when we first start speaking, and that's okay. Try to translate that nervous energy into enthusiasm, so that even if you feel anxious or shy, you still convey excitement about sharing your ideas with the people who showed up to hear them. For an example of an academic speaker who communicates energy and purpose, I recommend watching Dayu Lin's talk on the neuroscience of aggression, delivered to an audience of other experts. I've included a screenshot from the opening minutes of her talk (Figure 2), although to get the full effect, you need to watch her in action. Lin's demeanor offers

3. Patrick C. Friman, "Behavior Analysts to the Front! A 15-Step Tutorial on Public Speaking," *Behavioral Analyst* 37 (2014): 113. I'll add that it's important not to start by apologizing. It's an understandable impulse, one I often have but have learned to squash. I've seen many speakers begin by apologizing for rudimentary slides or lack of familiarity with the microphone. This undermines the speaker's authority. It also makes the audience feel as though they have to take care of the speaker. One way to minimize apologies is to follow the advice in chapter 6 about using slides effectively and in chapter 8 about arriving early to familiarize yourself with the technology in the room where you deliver your talk. Should you find yourself fumbling with the machinery at any point, that's okay. Take a beat and say, "Excuse me, I need some help." No need to apologize; it's normal to require some support when presenting in a venue you don't know well.

FIGURE 2. Screenshot from a talk by Dayu Lin, "The Neural Substrates for Aggression," January 2019. Image used with the permission of Dayu Lin and the Federation of European Neuroscience Societies.

a great model for how to speak in a fully academic mode while communicating passion for one's research and zeal about sharing its results. (She also has great slides.)[4]

The seasoned academics I interviewed all counseled easing into the first two or three minutes of a talk, in order to let the audience settle in. Mariana Alessandri cautioned that the "audience isn't really listening in your first sentence. . . . They're not ready. If you're using a key word, wait until the second, third, fourth, fifth sentence. Don't say it right away."[5] Late-

4. Dayu Lin, "The Neural Substrates for Aggression," Federation of European Neuroscience Societies Hertie Winter School 2018 on Neural Control of Instinctive and Innate Behaviour, Obergurgl, Austria, January 6–12, 2019, posted April 27, 2021, by @FENS, YouTube video, 42:44, https://www.youtube.com/watch?v=fZkHshEIp3s.

5. Robert Mawhinney made the same point: "The average audience member was just dealing with a problem with a graduate student or dealing with their child

comers are usually trickling in for the first few minutes, which is one reason speakers often begin by thanking people who've helped organize the event or contributed significantly to its content—sponsors and funders; archivists and librarians; advisees, postdocs, and collaborators. However, I don't recommend reading aloud a long list of people whom you'd like to thank unless you want to suck all the life out of the room. Lists, as the previous chapter pointed out, are boring. They're also difficult to memorize, which means you'd probably have to read that list off a piece of paper or a slide, which prevents you from making eye contact with your audience at the very moment when you most need to do so (see chapter 7).

Instead, consider keeping your opening thanks very brief and generic. While making eye contact with your audience, say, "I'd like to thank everyone who made it possible for me to be here today," and leave it at that. Or put some time into making your acknowledgments creative and edifying. Yale University religious studies professor Kathryn Lofton did this in the classiest way I've ever seen when she opened her talk by naming colleagues who had influenced her thinking, complete with capsule accounts of each person's scholarship.[6] Thanking others for their work also became a way for Lofton to describe her own intellectual interests and affiliations. The result combined the personal touch of a book's acknowledgments section with the intellectual overview of an annotated

at home"—they need a minute or two before they're ready to give your talk their full attention.

6. Kathryn Lofton, "Sensitive People: On Being Alive Today," Institute for Religion, Culture and Public Life, Columbia University, September 18, 2023.

bibliography or literature review. Because Lofton was thanking people she knew, it was easy for her to be vivid and specific. And because people are interested in people, her acknowledgments engaged our attention and had us feeling awake and alive when she shifted to the substance of her talk.

You'll decide what's best given the specific occasion and your personal preferences. If you do open with acknowledgments that take a minute or longer to deliver, adapt what Elisheva Baumgarten did when transitioning from giving thanks to giving her talk. Take a beat and then say, slowly and purposefully, while looking directly at your audience, "So let us begin."

Reading the Room

Sometimes it makes sense to begin your talk by asking your audience a question. It's a great way to foster connection and especially easy to do when delivering relatively interactive or informal talks. Some speakers begin by using the polling function in Zoom to ask the audience questions related to their talk topics. Or you can begin with a question: "How many of you here are theorists? How many are experimentalists?" If nothing else, it's fun to watch how people's entire demeanor changes when you address them directly and show an interest in who they are. When I give a talk on Johann von Goethe's novel *Wilhelm Meister's Apprenticeship,* I begin by noting that most of the colleagues I've polled have never read it. I then say something like, "So you're in great company if you haven't read *Meister* and very unusual if you have. How many people here have read the book from start to finish?" Usually about three people raise their hands. I then say, "Well, that confirms my point. Not to worry—I'll be supplying background information." Should I ever encounter an audience of *Meister* mavens, I will skip some of that background and dedicate the time saved to the question-and-answer session. If you're uncomfortable cutting material on the fly, annotate your script in advance to mark what you'd skip if your audience turns out to consist almost entirely of fellow specialists.

Opening Gambits

Examples

One excellent way to open is with an example. You can start with a well-known example and ask a new question about it: "For centuries, people have wondered about the enigmatic meaning of the Mona Lisa's smile, but this talk is going to show that we should also be asking questions about her hair." It's also effective to open with an example that no one else in the room is likely to know or expect. A surprising lab result, a little-known incident drawn from a historical document, or a surprising moment in an interview you conducted would all be engaging ways to make your research come alive. As discussed in the previous chapter, surprising examples activate your audience's attention. Introducing a piece of evidence that you know more about than anybody else will also help you feel authoritative and can boost your confidence at the start of your talk, when you probably need it most.

Another effective way to begin a talk is to show an image or clip that encapsulates your key claims, even if your work

FIGURE 3. Screenshot from a talk by Barbara Henry, "Road, River, and Book," January 26, 2021, depicting Isaak Levitan's *Vladimirka Road* (1892). Image used with the permission of Barbara Henry and the North American Dostoevsky Society.

doesn't focus on audiovisual media. Barbara Henry opened her talk on Russian literary underworlds by showing a slide of a painting of the road to Siberia and talking us through what it depicted (Figure 3). The pale road at the painting's center, "stretching before us into the measureless gray distance where sky and earth merge," anticipated the talk's thesis that writers like Dostoevsky saw the voyage to the underworld not as a descent into the depths but as a leveling experience that required trudging across an endless open road. Opening with an arresting image, as Henry did, unites the speaker with the audience and audience members with one another by having everyone focus intently on the same thing.[7]

7. Barbara Henry, "Road, River, and Book: The Russian Literary Underworld," Sawchen Lecture Series in Slavic Studies, Department of Central, Eastern, and

The ideal opening example both presents background information by setting the scene (who, what, where, when) and raises the question that the talk will answer. Bathsheba Demuth did this when she opened her talk "Do Whales Judge Us?" with a story about a recent conflict between an environmental activist and an Indigenous whale hunter. The story was inherently dramatic and intellectually compelling: a conflict over a charismatic megafauna where both opponents had valid claims. After telling the story, Demuth posed a key question that her anecdote raised and that her talk would answer: "How did we get to this impasse?" She then provided a road map by telling us she'd be answering that question by focusing on five groups over the past 150 years: three groups of whalers, one group of environmentalists, and whales themselves.[8]

Road Maps

The road maps mentioned in the previous chapter provide another excellent way to begin a talk. Here, for handy reference, is a road map to road maps. The order may vary, but these are the key points to cover at the outset:

Northern European Studies, University of British Columbia, and Bicentennial Speaker Series, 2020–21, North American Dostoevsky Society, January 26, 2021, posted March 19, 2021, by @North American Dostoevsky Society, YouTube video, 54:09, https://www.youtube.com/watch?v=utjsnbRq2HM.

8. Bathsheba Demuth, "Do Whales Judge Us? Interspecies History and Ethics," Environment Forum, Mahindra Humanities Center, Harvard University, November 6, 2019, posted December 5, 2019, by @Harvard University, YouTube video, 1:51:47, https://www.youtube.com/watch?v=yh_kJA0Naug.

- State your key question and place it within a larger context.
- Provide an overview of the current state of research in relevant subfields.
- Situate your work in these subfields by explaining what you thought you would learn from posing and answering your key question.
- State the hypothesis you tested or the thesis you are putting forward.
- Briefly describe the methods and evidence you used.
- Preview your key findings, and summarize what makes them original, surprising, and significant.

Robert Mawhinney advised addressing the following questions in a road map—and it can help to state them before answering them: "Where are we in this subfield? What do we think we know, why do we think we know it, and how solid is that knowledge?" Next, having explained *what* you're exploring, explain *why* you're exploring it. Are you trying to confirm what we think we already know? Are you trying to show we don't know something as well as we should? Are you aiming to identify what we should be studying but haven't been? Or perhaps there is a discrepancy you are trying to resolve, a gap you are trying to fill, or a synthesis you want to achieve.

Your road map can also explain what makes your key question interesting and significant and why you've been able to make progress where others haven't. Do you have a new method, instrument, technique, concept, theory, interpretation, or evidence? Have you improved on previous claims with new data, more accurate measurements, new sources, or fresh interpretations of old sources?

One final tip for your opening road map. If your talk forms part of a dissertation or book, it can be helpful to share a chapter list that pithily situates your talk in the larger project you're undertaking. This can also show that you've conceptualized your entire project even if you haven't yet written all of it, which can be helpful in some situations, especially job talks. Showing a table of contents implicitly invites people to ask questions about any and all of the chapters listed, so do this only if you're ready to talk about all the parts of your work.

Closing Statements

By the end of your talk, you're tired, and so is your audience. Perk them up by signaling that you're about to finish. As soon as you say, "In conclusion," "With that in mind, I'll close with," people snap to attention.

An adage about presentations in general also holds true for academic talks: first tell them what you're going to tell them, then tell it to them, then tell them what you've told them.

Here are some ways to signpost that you're about to tell people what you've told them:

- "To conclude, I hope I've shown that. . . ." At a bare minimum, conclude your talk by recapitulating your key claims and explaining what makes them significant. If you opened with a question, restate it and summarize how you've answered it. Or zoom out to end with an even bigger question than you began with, as literary critic Jennifer Wenzel did when she ended a talk on the wondrous and the ordinary in a world defined by fossil fuel use by asking, "What does it mean to make progress?"[9]

- "One final example before I conclude." Just as opening with an anecdote can work well, it can also be effective to close with one. While it's confusing to provide detailed discussions of new data, sources, or topics at the very end of a talk, it can be very clarifying to end with a fresh example that illustrates and encapsulates what you've already argued. If you find yourself juggling too many examples earlier in your talk and are having a hard time killing your darlings, consider moving one of your best examples to the conclusion.
- "I'll conclude, then, where I began."[10] An equally effective way to end: circle back to the example you

9. Jennifer Wenzel, "Between Petro-Magic and the Pedestrian," Environment Forum, Mahindra Humanities Center, Harvard University, October 20, 2021, posted November 2, 2021, by @Mahindra Humanities Center, YouTube video, 42:59, https://www.youtube.com/watch?v=V5RfI9vAwyI.

10. Shannon Jackson, "Ecological Time in Time-Based Media Art," Environment Forum, Mahindra Humanities Center, Harvard University, February 17, 2022, posted February 28, 2022, by @Mahindra Humanities Center, YouTube video, 1:17:20, https://www.youtube.com/watch?v=bkUP8bdwoaU. Mathematician Tamar Ziegler used the same move to conclude the talk "Sign Patterns of the Möbius Function": "I want to wrap up, and I'm coming back to the original question I started with." Tamar Ziegler, "Sign Patterns of the Möbius Function," Mathematics, Physics & Computer Science Series, Masaryk University, Brno, October 10, 2024, posted March 13, 2025, by @Muni Seminar Series, YouTube video, 55:35, https://www.youtube.com/watch?v=krTUFq8-z-U.

opened with and summarize how your talk has explained it or presented it in a new light.

- Gesture toward a different approach. If your talk has been theoretical, what would make it more empirical? If it's been empirical, what are the implications for theory? Rebecca Willett ended a talk on machine learning on this kind of speculative, self-reflexive note by mentioning that other researchers had recently taken her team's theoretical model and tested its applications.[11] Conversely, if your talk focuses on very specific case studies, you can finish by speculating about the more general points those case studies make.
- Conclude by looking to the future. Chemist Melanie Sanford wrapped up her talk by addressing new avenues her research opened: "I want to finish by leaving you with some preliminary results and opportunities to show what is possible with this chemistry."[12] In our interview, Robert Mawhinney offered a series of future-oriented questions one can raise when ending a talk. What might you need to do to further test and solidify your findings? How might you extend them to a broader

11. Rebecca Willett, "Learning Low-Rank Functions with Neural Networks," Yale Institute for Foundations of Data Science, Yale University, April 26, 2024, posted June 5, 2024, by @Yale FDS (Foundations of Data Science), YouTube video, 36:15, https://www.youtube.com/watch?v=VpTJEmoMqJw.

12. Melanie Sanford, "New Strategies for the C-H Functionalization of Aliphatic Amines," Center for Selective C-H Functionalization Virtual Symposium, National Science Foundation, July 28, 2015, posted by December 3, 2015, by @ Center for Selective C-H Functionalization, YouTube video, 28:08, https://www.youtube.com/watch?v=fFC4WuSbXdQ.

> context? What's the potential relevance to other subfields or to your discipline as a whole? Which of the questions you've raised that day remain unanswered and open, and what new questions emerge from the material you've presented?

I'll end this section on endings by quoting Elisheva Baumgarten's exemplary conclusion to her talk on medieval Jewish prayers:

> I'll end with both a definitive statement and a question. I began with a rabbi who objected to Jews praying like Christians and ended with a rabbi who repurposed a Christian prayer for Jews. So we are left with a question of how Jews decided what to take and not take from Christian culture and how it could and could not be used. This is an issue that anyone here who thinks about contacts between cultures would be interested in.

Baumgarten began her conclusion by signposting that her talk was about to end, then signposted her reasoning process by identifying her closing statement as having a definitive component and a speculative one. Her next sentence juxtaposes her starting point ("I began with") and her closing example ("and ended with") in a way that elegantly summarizes the argument and arc of her entire talk. After restating her finding—that Jews decided *what* to take and not take from Christian culture—Baumgarten identified that future research could ask *how* Jews made those decisions. The two final sentences zoom out to offer the broadest possible context for her talk, inviting those in the audience who may not have been specifically interested in medieval European religions to think about what this specific case study might teach scholars about cultural contact in general.[13]

To sum up: make your titles inviting and your introductions brief. Take the stage deliberately and confidently. Make eye contact with your audience when delivering the first lines of your talk, and communicate with enthusiasm and energy.

The opening of your talk can begin with a question or a vivid example and should offer a road map.

Just before you conclude, tell people that you're about to do so. You can end by circling back to an opening example or by presenting one final piece of compelling evidence. Don't, however, end a talk with a flurry of new data, sources, concepts, or claims.

When wrapping up, sum up the most important questions the talk asked and the most significant answers it provided. Other effective final moves involve anticipating objections, naming open questions, and identifying the broadest possible contexts for your research—all of which pave the way for the question-and-answer session, covered in the next chapter.

13. Elisheva Baumgarten, "Shared Appeals to Different Gods: Jews, Christians and Medieval Prayer," Helen Diller Distinguished Annual Lecture, Center for Jewish Studies, University of California, Berkeley, February 21, 2023, posted March 11, 2023, by @Berkeley Center for Jewish Studies, YouTube video, 1:19:48, https://www.youtube.com/watch?v=904TwPbA7b0.

5

The Q&A

I HAVE good news and I have bad news.

I'll start with the bad news, because it isn't really news. You are probably one of the many people who find fielding questions the scariest part of giving an academic talk. Why? Because it's unpredictable. You can plan exactly what you will say in your talk, but you can never know for certain what questions you will have to field or who will ask them.

The stakes are high because how you field questions plays an outsized role in how people judge your performance. A lackluster question-and-answer session (Q&A) can undermine an excellent talk. A brilliant Q&A can salvage a flawed one, because how you answer questions completes the work of the talk itself: to convince people of your specific arguments and overall expertise. You might succeed; you might fail. People are watching to see which it will be, and they will be talking to each other later about how you did. It's understandable that even academics who love being in the spotlight and thrive on receiving critical feedback often feel a twinge of apprehension as they wrap up their presentation and wait for someone to raise a hand.

The good news is related to the bad news. The unpredictable is inherently dramatic. People often feel that they would have gotten more out of reading a talk than hearing it delivered, but they rarely say that they would have rather asked their questions over email. Indeed, the opportunity to pose questions and hear them answered in real time is a key reason academics attend talks.

Theater professor David Levine noted in our interview that the Q&A is the one part of an academic talk that engages everyone, because during the Q&A, we are witnessing someone thinking in the moment. The speaker's delivery usually improves, because "most people come alive when they are defending" a position or connecting with their audience. Department members notorious for nodding off during talks usually wake up when questions get underway. The energy in the room changes.

I once witnessed a speaker whose delivery of her prepared remarks felt disengaged and flat but who sparkled when delivering extemporaneous answers to a question that drew on her workplace experience. Describing what would happen when a staff member would finally talk to her about a problem that she, as a supervisor, hadn't realized existed, she riffed: "You think, 'Oh my god, why have we been doing that?' I call these the insanity moments." While answering a question, the speaker became fully present in a way that improved what she said and how she said it. She even coined a phrase, "insanity moments," that would have been a great sound bite to add to future versions of her presentation.

All this drama, so thrilling for the audience, makes it stressful for the speaker to perform the work of demonstrating expertise. As Levine observed, the speaker is *defending* a position. Of course, at its best, the Q&A is, as physicist Robert Mawhinney put it, "a conversation, not a contest," but we've all seen Q&A sessions that verged on the gladiatorial. Especially for graduate students giving their first talks, the Q&A seems, as philosopher Mariana Alessandri put it, like "the 'gotcha' part."

Seems like—and sometimes is. Difficult situations do arise, and it's normal to feel apprehensive about how you will handle them. People will ask questions that aren't really questions. They will press you about things you know little or nothing about, some relevant, some not, and ask you to comment on examples you don't have at your command. They will challenge your choice of theory, method, and examples. Some questioners will even sound rude, hostile, or patronizing. None of these challenges can be addressed by painstakingly rehearsing bulletproof responses in advance, because you never know exactly what questioners will do. All of this is even more nerve-racking if you are presenting in English and it is neither your first language nor the first language of many in the audience, a common situation in many disciplines.

But here's the best news of all: the situation is not as unpredictable as you may fear. You *can* prepare in advance, and this chapter will explain how.

The Purpose of an Academic Q&A

To answer questions effectively, it helps to keep in mind why talks include Q&A sessions at all and even consider them so important that organizers often allot equal time to the Q&A and to the presentation itself. Some departments even tell speakers to allot *more* time to the Q&A, especially for job talks.

The Q&A has two purposes, one specific, one more sweeping.

The specific purpose of the Q&A is to give people the chance to engage with the material you presented. They came to learn, and they will ask questions designed to help them better understand what you said. Because they are academics, they also came to teach. In that spirit, audience members will pose questions designed to help you strengthen your claims and reasoning, often by pointing out flaws or weaknesses.

The more sweeping purpose of the Q&A is to help people in the audience assess you as a thinker and as a colleague. On this score, the Q&A is more informative than the talk itself: you had hours to polish your talk, often with help from colleagues, advisors, and friends. But people also want a sense of how you would respond to students asking challenging questions or colleagues stopping you in the hall to chat about a knotty research problem. The Q&A offers insights about what you're like when it is just you, thinking on your feet, and you don't get to phone a friend. I did once witness an eminent senior scholar who was being grilled by a graduate student throw up his hands and turn to that student's advisor and ask *her* to answer for him. She did, but shunting the question to someone else in the audience didn't make a good impression. Academic inquiry is a collective effort, but when it comes to the Q&A, you are on your own.

For that reason, many people believe that the Q&A reveals a lot about the speaker's intellect. Questioners will be observing how flexibly and capaciously someone thinks when presented with alternative interpretations or contradictory evidence. How deep is the presenter's knowledge? Do they know only about the cases they presented, or do they have more examples on tap? What about breadth? Can they extend their findings to other contexts—a different organism, another historical period? Can they offer compact, logical, nuanced answers to tough questions?

The Q&A also reveals personal character and helps the audience imagine what the speaker might be like as a colleague and teacher. Are they passionate about their material and good at communicating its significance? When they don't know something, or get something wrong (as everyone does, on occasion), do they get defensive or forthrightly admit their ignorance or mistakes? Do they respond well to feedback and make the most of constructive criticism? Are they interested in other people's ideas as well as their own? Can they assert themselves tactfully and be generous and gracious even when their interlocutors are not?

To understand the purpose of an academic Q&A, it also helps to distinguish how academic answers differ from other kinds. A good reference point for this is a talk Gita Gopinath gave as part of the University of Glasgow's distinguished Adam Smith lecture series.[1] Gopinath's fascinating presentation applied Smith's ideas, generated at the time of the

1. Gita Gopinath, "The Power and Perils of the 'Artificial Hand': Considering AI Through the Ideas of Adam Smith," University of Glasgow, June 5, 2023, IMF Videos video, 1:04:41, https://www.imf.org/en/News/Articles/2023/06/05/sp060523-fdmd-ai-adamsmith.

eighteenth-century industrial revolution, to the twenty-first-century revolution in artificial intelligence. Gopinath has a PhD in economics from Princeton and was a professor of economics at Harvard, so she has considerable academic experience, but when she gave this talk, she was the first deputy managing director of the International Monetary Fund (IMF). When answering questions, she spoke from that extra-academic position. Her main purpose was to represent the IMF in the best possible light, not to demonstrate her academic expertise or even to convince the audience of her arguments.

Speaking as a representative of a political institution, Gopinath gave *politic* answers, not academic ones. She reframed every question to make it about the IMF's mission, values, and policies. For example, when asked what did and didn't work about an IMF initiative to end poverty during the COVID-19 epidemic, Gopinath responded by changing the question to "How would what we did there inflect how IMF approaches AI?" This was both a valid return to the topic of her talk and a way to reframe past errors as paving the way for future improvement. Watching her respond to that question and others, I inferred that her two chief aims when answering questions were to demonstrate her skill at leading a powerful global institution and to assure her audience of that institution's merits.

Politic answers are clear, simple, reassuring, and often graciously evasive. Academic answers address questions directly and are nuanced, complex, and wide-ranging. Academic answers should demonstrate expertise and the speaker's ability to defend and refine their claims, while communicating enthusiasm about the talk's topic and interest in other people's knowledge and points of view. Politic answers pivot deftly back to the speaker's key talking points. Do that as an academic, and you will be dismissed as limited or glib. As an academic, your job is to explore ramifications, delve into details, and be judicious about when to complicate matters and when to simplify them. When giving an academic answer, it's more than okay to be mildly combative and wander into some byways. It's academia, after all—we are all about getting into the weeds.

With this in mind, let's turn to where your Q&A starts: with your talk itself.

Setting Up the Q&A in Your Talk

You can't know in advance exactly who will ask what. But just as musicians prepare for a jam session by practicing scales, chords, and rhythms until these become habitual, you can prepare for the Q&A in two ways: by practicing answers to questions you can anticipate and by using a judicious blend of pruning and planting in your talk itself.

The next section addresses how to answer questions, but let's start with how your presentation itself can set up the questions you will get. A cardinal rule of any talk is **never to go over your time limit**. That usually means that as you revise your outline or script, you'll find yourself pruning a lot of material. In gardening, pruning often involves trimming some healthy leaves and branches, as well as dead or diseased ones, in order to help plants flourish. You can create propitious conditions for your Q&A not only by removing the duller or less essential bits but also by cutting some relevant and interesting material or reducing it to a quick mention. If you're reading a text aloud, this can be a good occasion for the ad-libbing mentioned in chapter 2: "Here's a point I don't have room to discuss in the talk itself but can answer questions about later."

It's counterintuitive but true: removing some of your best material sets you up for questions you are fully prepared to answer well. One great example of this in my corpus is the talk film studies professor Jaimie Baron gave about filmmaker Shirley Clark.[2] Baron kept her talk to thirty-five minutes while presenting a book-length project, so I'm guessing she took an expert scalpel to her first draft. During the Q&A, the audience asked about things Baron could have included in her presentation but wisely hadn't: How did you first come across Clark? Can you go into more detail about how other scholars have discussed her work? What has her legacy been? Whom did she influence? How did her reception differ in the United States and in Europe? Can you say more about how her filmmaking style relates to the aesthetics of the jazz musicians she collaborated with? Those would all have been great topics to include in the talk itself, but doing so would have forced Baron to go into less detail about her chosen examples. Instead, she wisely adhered to the academic preference for depth over breadth and trusted that her Q&A would become an extension of her talk. It hurts to cut juicy, relevant material from the presentation itself, but doing so sets up the Q&A as an annex for your outtakes. You're not killing your darlings: you're placing them in a waiting room.

2. Jaimie Baron, "Countering Culture: Shirley Clarke and the Edges of Cinema," Radcliffe Institute for Advanced Study at Harvard University, March 29, 2023, posted April 6, 2023, by @Harvard Radcliffe Institute, YouTube video, 59:19, https://www.youtube.com/watch?v=YUqEnb6HkUE.

Pruning is especially challenging—and necessary—for those presenting a portion of a dissertation or book. Often, it's important to give a sense of the larger project, but if you go into too much detail, you lose time needed to give the smaller extract its due. A good solution is to prompt someone to ask, in the Q&A, "How does what you presented today relate to the larger project from which it's drawn?" To set up that question, I recommend *mentioning*, not explaining, the pieces you are not including that day. As I suggested in chapter 4, an easy way to do this is to show a slide of the table of contents of your dissertation or book and say, "This talk is drawn from a larger project; here's a list of chapters." This plants the seeds for a question you will find very easy to answer: "How does [insert a claim your talk developed] play out in the rest of your project?" While you may be tempted to say a sentence about each of the chapters of the book from which your talk is drawn, I urge you not to do that. It's great to evoke the larger *framework* that unites all of the chapters. But a single sentence about each chapter will satisfy no one, and more than that will dilute your talk's focus. Show the slide, say nothing, and set yourself up to sound erudite and in command when audience members ask later about other portions of your project that you have thought about in your dissertation abstract, book proposal, and grant applications.

Pruning, in other words, is actually a form of sowing. By cutting material, you plant questions about what you excised. You can make this explicit in your talk itself. Have more to say about a particular example but need to move on to stay within your time limit? "There's a lot more I can say about this, and I'm happy to do so during the Q&A." Want to relate the particular topic you're presenting to a larger research program?

Say exactly that: "If people have questions about future directions and next steps for this research, we can discuss that during the Q&A." While I don't recommend saying this more than three times per talk, it's a useful rhetorical tool, especially if you are nervous about cutting a point that you think some people will expect you to address.

Another good way to plant seeds for your Q&A is to mention additional examples you could discuss. One of the most common questions at an academic talk is "What about [insert example]?" Usually that example is one the person asking the question knows inside and out but the speaker may not. I once gave a talk on female friendship in Victorian novels that opened by discussing a scene from George Eliot's *Middlemarch*. During the Q&A, another specialist in Victorian literature asked me, "What about *Romola*?" It was a fair question, even though *Romola* is one of Eliot's more obscure works. I had even read *Romola*, but I couldn't remember it very well. As the next section addresses, you should never pretend to know something you don't, so I answered honestly and with an attempt at humor:

> You know, I read that novel, but years ago, during a very long and very hot train ride, and all I remember is how boring I found it. I can say more about how my ideas play out in some other Eliot novels, and I'd be interested in hearing you say more about how you think *Romola* relates to my talk.

The questioner did just that, but I still had nothing to add, so I responded by talking about Eliot's final novel, *Daniel Deronda*. Still, my lack of knowledge became a thing, and the next questioner said, "Not to *Romola* you, but can you talk about whether your argument holds for Elizabeth Barrett Browning's *Aurora Leigh*?" As it happened, that was one of my outtakes, and I could. Phew.

I could not have prepared in advance to answer the *Romola* question itself, but I could have better set up my talk to reduce the chances of someone asking it. While it would have been excessive to prep for the Q&A by rereading every novel George Eliot ever wrote, it would have been smart to end my discussion of *Middlemarch* by saying, "I'd be happy to say more later about how what I've been discussing also helps us think about *Daniel Deronda* and *The Mill on the Floss*," both considered more major texts than *Romola*. Odds are good that someone asking about an additional George Eliot novel would then have asked me to talk about the one I had already earmarked for further discussion. If they'd said, "What about *Romola*?," I would have been better set up to say, "I haven't really thought about *Romola* in this context, but as I said, I can talk about how these ideas play out in two of Eliot's other major works." Some questions are softballs, not because they are easy but because you have already set yourself up to field them. If you want that kind of softball question, lob it to the audience during your talk, and hope someone tosses it back to you later.

Conversely, don't invite curveballs. Never introduce a concept or example you are not prepared to discuss in depth. As art historian Branden Joseph put it, "Know your material. All of it." This is especially the case if the protocol in your discipline is to ask questions throughout the talk, which often happens in economics and political science. I once saw a political science talk go off the rails after only five minutes because the speaker didn't have his examples down cold. Early on, he mentioned a particular politician's loss of an election as an example of single-issue voting. When asked how he knew that this issue was the only one that people had based their votes on, he had no answer ready. A few minutes later, he evoked an example that referred to eight roll call votes and listed three or four of them. Someone interrupted to ask what the others were; he couldn't remember. Oof.

To sum up, your talk will set up a good Q&A if you

- Prune relevant material to leave room for your audience to ask about it,
- Plant seeds by flagging what you can discuss in more detail after your talk ends,
- Know your examples inside and out (no gardening metaphors here, just do it).

Answering Questions: What to Expect

The Q&A is improvised, but as noted above, you can, and should, walk into your talk already prepared with answers to a host of questions your audience will likely ask. If you're presenting about a larger project, someone will likely ask about other elements of it. People will ask you to apply your arguments to other cases, so have some other cases to hand or explain why your points don't carry over to other situations.

Audience members will ask you to explain further why you selected the examples you did and how you found them. If there's a historical dimension to what you're discussing, they will ask about what came before and after. If there's a quantitative dimension to what you're discussing, they will ask for more details about how you measure it. Some people will ask for causal explanations—about *why* what you have presented is the case. They may want to hear more about how your work builds on or revises previous scholarship or influential theoretical frameworks. People will present alternative analyses of your materials, some of which you can anticipate. They will ferret out unarticulated assumptions and apparent contradictions and challenge you to defend or resolve them.

Formulate these types of questions in advance of giving your talk, and practice answering them on your own, out loud, using complete sentences. When you rehearse your talk for friends (when, not if—see chapter 8), include a long Q&A session. Make sure your test audience includes someone blunt and tactless—that friend (we all have at least one) who often blurts out what many people are thinking but are too shy or polite to say. The blurter may well ask the question you most fear answering, in its harshest form: "Isn't this all just basically a rehash of Noam Chomsky?" It's best to grapple with that question in a practice session so that you're not encountering it for the first time when delivering your talk for real.

Answering Questions: Dos and Don'ts

You have concluded your talk and received your applause. At this point, the moderator may ask if you are willing to entertain questions. The answer is always, "Yes, I'm happy to." The moderator will then call on people or check for questions in the Zoom chat. Sometimes there is no moderator or the moderator forgets to do their job. In that case, after concluding and pausing, you should say, "I'm now happy to answer questions."

If you're using a projector, I recommend turning it off when your talk ends, so that the sound of the fan doesn't muffle questioners and you're not caught in the projector's glare as you move around. You can always momentarily turn it back on if you need to show a slide. If you absolutely have to keep the projector on during your entire Q&A, stay out of its path—you may be able to tolerate the light glaring on you, but it's disruptive for the audience.

Don't be nervous if there are no immediate questions (see below). Conversely, if many hands shoot up all at once, it can be effective to say, "Oh, this is great, so many questions—I'm going to gather a few before I start to answer them." Since that's not the default convention, don't do this if you are a very junior scholar, but I've seen moderators and senior scholars bundle questions to excellent effect. It's a great way to give more people a chance to engage with the speaker, and it lets you as speaker choose which question you'd like to answer first.

The following are some blanket "dos" for answering questions.

Do keep your answers compact. Historian Daniel Immerwahr recounted in our interview that someone once decided to count how many questions he'd answered after a talk: twenty-three, which means each of his answers averaged about one and a half minutes. If you think that's impossibly brief, keep in mind that the Beatles song "Eleanor Rigby" is just a little over two minutes long and covers a lot of ground. You don't need to limit yourself to a specific amount of time, but keep in mind that short answers will allow you to field more questions. That makes it more likely that everyone who wants to ask a question can—which is the least you can do for folks who took time to listen to your talk. Keeping answers short and fielding more questions can also make you seem confident and promote connection between you and your audience. Finally, keeping answers closer in length to the questions themselves makes the Q&A feel more like a conversation. As Immerwahr observed, the Q&A should feel like a genuine back-and-forth, not like "dueling monologues."

Do very briefly summarize each question before answering it. Often, many audience members can't hear the question, and if they don't know what the question was, they're going to have trouble making sense of your answer. Your summaries of audience questions can be terse: "This is a question about benzenes." I'm going to stress this point because academic speakers rarely summarize the questions they field and they should. At one talk I attended, after each question, I heard people around me murmur, "What was the question?" But no one said that loudly enough for the speaker to hear. Repeating the question is especially important if your talk is being recorded because the recording equipment often picks up the speaker but not audience members. Even when moderators hand audience members microphones, there's always someone in the room who didn't catch the whole question. Don't bother to ask if everyone heard the question, because not everyone who missed it will say so. Conversely, if you're the person asking a question, keep in mind that it helps everyone if you speak loudly and slowly.

Do perform listening attentively. Audiences tend to look at the speaker while someone asks a question. If you're the speaker, it's good form to demonstrate respect and interest by looking directly at each questioner, nodding, and smiling slightly if that's part of your expressive repertoire, all things Alison Pugh did in the Q&A following her talk on affective labor.[3] Posing questions is an act of service to the speaker, and questioners can feel as vulnerable as speakers. For these reasons, and simply because it's courteous, it's best to field questions hospitably and graciously. Remember that your task in the Q&A is not just to show how smart you are but to make your audience feel smart, too.

Do move around while answering questions. As I discuss in chapter 7, it's good to gesture and move around a bit while delivering your talk. During the Q&A, you're often free to be even more mobile. If you can, move closer to the audience when responding to questions. Use gestures, especially if you didn't gesture much while delivering your talk. Unless test audiences have told you that you are too antic, trust that whatever you do will stay within the ideal bounds of what Nicholas Dames called "restrained dynamism." As he pointed out in our interview, it's almost never the case that academic speakers move too much and almost always the case that we stand too stiffly. Moving freely is helpful because it makes you seem comfortable, nondefensive, and engaged, which makes a good impression and puts your audience at ease. For a great example of someone using gestures to excellent effect when

3. Allison Pugh, "The Stratification of Human Contact: The Present and Future of Connective Labour," 2022/2023 Distinguished Speaker Series, Department of Sociology, University of British Columbia, September 6, 2022, https://sociology.ubc.ca/news/watch-dr-allison-pughs-distinguished-speaker-lecture/.

answering questions, I recommend watching the Q&A for art historian Joseph Koerner's talk on artist Albrecht Dürer. Even when seated, which intrinsically restrains one's range of motion, Koerner used his hands in ways that punctuated his points and made his delivery feel expressive and energetic.[4]

Finally, when answering questions, move a bit (just a bit) closer to the person who asked them, but maintain eye contact with the whole room. Everyone should feel involved in your answer, not just the person who asked the question.

Do make sure that the content of your answers goes beyond the content of your talk. This is especially important for junior scholars giving job talks, where many of the people posing the questions are assessing your future potential as a researcher. If all your answers repeat the ideas and examples you already presented in the talk itself, it makes your knowledge seem very limited. If you've followed my earlier advice and pruned some of your best material, it will be easy for you to dazzle your audience during the Q&A with answers that range beyond what you've already presented.

Do align how you answer questions with how you deliver your talk. No one expects you to answer questions in exactly the same way as you deliver your talk, but you should aim for continuity. People use the Q&A to assess your character, and aligning your writerly and conversational styles reinforces your credibility. I started out by saying that most people's delivery improves when they start answering questions, but some people

4. Joseph Koerner, "Dürer's Mobility," 2021 Linbury Lecture, National Gallery, January 14, 2022, posted March 7, 2022, by @The National Gallery, YouTube video, 1:34:52, https://www.youtube.com/watch?v=FqsCni1i9AY.

speak far less effectively once they step away from their scripts. I've seen people who delivered their talks at the right volume become inaudible when answering questions. Lots of speakers, when answering questions, pepper their speech with verbal tics: "you know," "right?," "like," "um," or a nervous laugh at the end of each sentence. Some people don't mind these tics, but many find them distracting at best, poor speaking at worst. I've noticed that when I answer questions, I tend to link all my sentences with "so" and "and," producing responses that seem to flow on and on like rivers. It's a bad habit because full stops articulate logical breaks and give the audience micro-rests that help them focus. I would never use run-on sentences in a written text, so I have worked to eliminate them from my speech. Chapter 7 offers advice about how to practice eliminating moves that you'd never deploy in writing.

Do be explicit about how your answers draw on other people's work. Always give credit where it's due when answering a question to which you don't have original answers. Brodwyn Fischer modeled this impeccably when answering a question this way: "Other people have researched that issue more deeply than I have, so what I'm about to tell you is what I've read in other people's books."[5]

Do make the questioner feel smart. Many of the experts I spoke with emphasized that your answers shouldn't just prove that *you're* smart. They should also make the questioner

5. Brodwyn Fischer, "Intimate Inequalities," Radcliffe Institute for Advanced Study at Harvard University, September 26, 2022, posted March 31, 2023, by @Harvard Radcliffe Institute, YouTube video, 59:51, https://www.youtube.com/watch?v=0TGMm6LASrU.

feel smart. I don't recommend doing this by simply saying, "That's a great question," which is blandly formulaic and can come off as sycophantic or patronizing. Instead, foreground precisely what makes the question valuable: "That question gets at a key issue at stake in this research, which is X."

Do answer the question, but also answer the question behind the question. Always answer the question directly and clearly, or admit that you can't (see below for how to handle that scenario). But don't limit yourself to the literal question. Your job is to demonstrate that you can think big, in conceptual terms, on the fly, and to show that you understand how your work relates to other work in your field or discipline.

People are more interested in how you think than in what you know. If someone asks how your argument about Beethoven's Fifth Symphony applies to Brahms's Fourth, don't focus exclusively on comparing the key changes in each symphony's final movement. Think out loud about what the question implies, and answer those questions, too. How did Romanticism change over the course of the nineteenth century? How did innovations in auditorium acoustics influence orchestration? Where was each composer in his career when composing the symphonies under discussion? Your audience will enjoy hearing you unfold all these possibilities, and you can cover each in a sentence or two, knowing someone will follow up if they want you to expand on a particular point. As Nicholas Dames put it, the Q&A "is not a deposition. You're allowed to be a bit free with how you answer the question because what you're trying to understand is the motive behind it."

Do feel free to disagree with the premise of a question. If you take issue with the assumption grounding a question, say so. Let's say someone asks a question about why you used quantitative methods instead of qualitative ones, and you don't see them as opposed. In a friendly but firm tone, respond something like this: "That question assumes that quantitative analysis doesn't include qualitative elements. I disagree. Here's why, and here's how that plays out in my research." This can be scary to do if you are a graduate student giving a job talk, but that's potentially where it is most important to demonstrate that you are an independent thinker who is ready to be a full colleague. I wouldn't reject the premise of a question more than once per talk, unless the situation absolutely demands it; you don't want to seem oppositional or resistant to feedback. But don't be afraid to disagree directly if the question warrants it. Asserting yourself when you have a genuinely important intellectual point to make tells people you are a mature scholar—and a bit of a maverick.

Do try to end your Q&A with a bang. Often, a moderator will say, "We can take one more question," so as a speaker, you will know when you are giving your last answer. Try to have a sound bite prepared that works as a concluding pronouncement. J. Mijin Cha ended the Q&A for her talk on decarbonization with this powerful phrase: "We are the ones who get to write the future. The future is not written, and we get to choose."[6] Barbara Henry ended her presentation on

6. J. Mijin Cha, "Just Transition or Just a Transition?: The Importance of Power, Organizing, and Framing in Decarbonization," Society of Fellows and Heyman Center for the Humanities, Columbia University, April 25, 2023, posted April 27,

underworlds in Russian literature with this elegant zinger, which could have worked equally well at the close of a Q&A: "Since escape is no longer possible, the challenge now is not to leave the underworld but to live in it. At least we have a guide."[7] It won't always be possible to close your Q&A that eloquently, but have a phrase in mind that allows you to send people off by reminding them what your point has been and where your research is going.

Things Not to Do When Answering Questions

Don't thank people for a question or praise it. People do this all the time. "Thank you for that question." "That's a great question." "I love that question." In my opinion, they should stop. And it's not just my opinion. Maybe this kind of thing works for a press conference, but academics don't like it. Many of the experts I interviewed volunteered, unprompted, that these phrases bug them. Let's break down why. First, it's filler, so it keeps answers from being compact. Second, it sounds rote, which makes the person saying it sound less sincere. Third, and most damagingly, it's evaluative. As Alessandri put it, it's "fake respect." Even praise is a judgment, and any

2023, by @SOFHeyman, YouTube video, 1:06:49, https://www.youtube.com/watch?v=bO1KlU0ovJQ.

7. Barbara Henry, "Road, River, and Book: The Russian Literary Underworld," Sawchen Lecture Series in Slavic Studies, Department of Central, Eastern, and Northern European Studies, University of British Columbia, and Bicentennial Speaker Series, 2020–21, North American Dostoevsky Society, January 26, 2021, posted March 19, 2021, by @North American Dostoevsky Society, YouTube video, 54:09, https://www.youtube.com/watch?v=utjsnbRq2HM.

judgment, even a positive one, asserts dominance. At best, Alessandri said when we talked about this, "it's a distancing move," when "what you're trying to do is pull them in and connect." If you really want to underscore that you like a question, don't just say *that* you like it; say *why*. I saw sociology professor Alison Pugh do this very effectively when she started an answer this way: "That's a great question because it reflects the concerns of the literature."[8]

Do not look or act uncomfortable. Avoid crossing your arms tightly, putting your hands on a chair or in your pockets, twiddling your hair, biting your nails, or clicking your pen. You may be doing these things to self-soothe (I know I do), but it signals lack of confidence in yourself and lack of ease with your audience, and some people find these actions and movements very distracting.[9]

Do not introduce new material when questions are done. Never hold your audience captive. At one talk I attended, after thirty minutes of Q&A, the moderator asked if there were any more questions. There weren't. Great! Time to check phones, use the bathroom, have a snack, go home, or get ready to teach. But no: the speaker decided, *after the audience made clear they had no more questions*, to introduce a new point by showing a slide containing a very long quote that he then read aloud and discussed for five solid minutes. Bad move. Even if people loved your talk, they also love leaving it.

8. Pugh, "Stratification of Human Contact."

9. See the lists of distracting body movements in Reinhart, *Giving Academic Presentations*, 18; and Anderson, *TED Talks*, 153, 207.

This is not live music, and you are not the Rolling Stones; no one is clamoring for an encore.

How to Handle Nightmare Scenarios

The three biggest fears people have about the questions they will be asked about their academic talk are these: What if there are no questions? What if someone asks me something I can't answer? What if someone is rude to me?

What if there are no questions? This fear is easy to deal with because it never happens. There are always people in the room who understand that it's their duty when attending lectures to ask questions and who will rise to the occasion if others do not. Sometimes, it might take a solid minute or two for someone to ask the first question. That will indeed feel very long to everyone, especially you, but trust me, the questions will arrive.

Hold back from comments that express discomfort about the wait; it's good to model that you are at ease with the thoughtful silences that often crop up when we teach small discussion-based courses. People need time to formulate good questions; give it to them. The smartest people in the room often wait a while to ask their questions. Don't interpret the wait as a sign that your talk didn't interest your audience. I've seen many excellent talks with ultimately lively Q&A sessions that got off to a slow start.

If the silence goes on for more than forty-five seconds, it can be effective for you to say (especially if you're a senior scholar) that you are happy to start by taking basic questions about the material you presented. For example, an art historian might say, "While people are thinking about what they'd like to ask, I'm happy to take basic questions about any of the images that I showed."

What if someone asks me something I can't answer? This, on the other hand, almost always happens. As noted earlier, you should not present material you don't know cold, but no one can know everything, even about their chosen topic, and many people will ask questions about their area of expertise, not yours. Even the most accomplished scholars can't offer perfect answers to every question. No one will judge you too harshly when this happens, so long as you adhere to the following strategies.

Never pretend to know something you don't. Most academics have strong bullshit detectors, and they respect people who don't try to bullshit. If you don't know the answer, say, "I don't know. I'll have to think about that more," and then talk about why the question matters and how different answers would affect your argument (understand the question behind the question). Remember, always, that academics are more interested in how you think than in what you know.

Sometimes you can't answer because you literally didn't hear the question. If you couldn't hear the person, say so, and ask them to repeat themselves a bit louder. Sometimes the questioner has an accent that you have trouble parsing. A tactful way to handle that situation, especially if you're in a large auditorium, can be this: "I caught some of your question but not all of it because the acoustics in here aren't great. Please find me after the talk and I'll answer you then." Or ask the person to email you their question, as computer scientist Moshe Y. Vardi did during the Q&A on his talk on efficiency and resilience.[10] It's a graceful way to address a common problem in polyglot intellectual communities that rely on a single language as a lingua franca.

Sometimes you can't answer because you didn't fully understand the question. In that case, say: "I'm sorry, I didn't quite understand the question, can you rephrase it?" Other ways to respond in this case include "Could you say more?" or "I want to make sure I understand your question—did you mean X?"

Sometimes people make comments that aren't really questions. They'll even say that: "This is more of a comment than a question." You can respond by politely saying, "I can respond to the comment, but first I want to check if you want to rephrase it as a question?" If that feels like too heavy a lift in some situations, remember, it's a conversation, not a contest, and conversations don't always involve pointed questions. Focus on the aspect of the comment you have the most to say about and address that: "Here's what that comment about X brings to mind."

Sometimes you can't answer because the answer lies outside your specialized knowledge. Many people like to ask about how your work relates to theirs. As I discuss below, in the section on how to be a good audience member, that's not always a good way to formulate questions, but it's a common move. If you don't immediately see how a question relates to your talk, it's valid to respond by cordially asking the

10. Moshe Y. Vardi, "Efficiency, Resilience, and Artificial Intelligence," Computer Science/Discrete Mathematics Seminar, Institute for Advanced Study, March 24, 2025, posted March 24, 2025, by @Institute for Advanced Study, YouTube video, 1:13:57, https://www.youtube.com/watch?v=Ji84f7eLxpU.

questioner to elaborate before you answer. The questioner says: "You just gave a talk about golf balls. I work on cheese soufflés. How does this relate to cheese soufflés?" You reply: "Cheese soufflés are not my expertise, so I haven't thought about that connection. Can you say a bit more about what makes you think about cheese soufflés in this context, and then I can tell you more about how I see that playing out with respect to golf balls?" Don't make people feel bad, but don't stand there struggling to meet the questioner entirely on their terrain—get them to meet you halfway.

When asked about something you know little or nothing about, **identify the portion of the question that you can answer by pivoting to what you do know**. Branden Joseph tells his graduate students to begin answering any question they don't immediately know the answer to this way: "We know X, Y, and Z, but I actually don't know the answer to [actual question]. It's an interesting question because that would open up A, B, and C." Another option is to say how you'd go about finding the answer: "I can't answer that now, but I would find the answer by looking in these archives/obtaining this data/deploying these methods/applying this theory/constructing this experiment."

Even if you can't answer the question itself, you can and should demonstrate that you understand its stakes: what makes it interesting, the ideas and paths it generates. If someone asks you how X relates to Y, and you don't have an instant response, say: "That makes me think about how X relates to Z. I haven't researched Y, but this is how I'd go about it and what I'd be thinking about if I did." What you say first sets a tone and is often what people remember best, so even when you can't answer the exact question, start with what you do know. While you should always state up-front if there is a specific point of fact you don't know, most questions you can't answer readily won't be about specific points of fact. In those cases, begin with a pivot, not least to buy yourself time to think. If you start talking about what you *know* you know, you may find you also have something to say about what you thought you didn't know.

Finally, keep in mind that **no one expects you to answer every question definitively**. Your Q&A should prove that you are smart, make questioners feel smart, and demonstrate that you will use the discussion to improve your project. When audience members ask you about something you didn't already think of, answering receptively makes them feel good about how much they know and how helpful they are being. I once saw a junior scholar giving a job talk respond to a multipart question by answering the components he could and then calmly saying, about the one portion he couldn't address, "I don't know the answer to that part of your question. I'll have to think about that more." He got the job.

It is also okay to be exploratory rather than authoritative: "I'm not absolutely sure of my answer, but if I gave it a try, this is what it might look like." Academics value flexibility of mind more than certainty and might even not like it if you answer every question definitively, especially if you are at the beginning of a project. What they want to see is that you are interested in the problems they raise and are going to take them on and think them through. In our interview, Daniel Immerwahr described a job talk where an audience member asked the speaker a "devastating" question. He still remembered how the speaker responded:

> Let me restate the question, and state its value, why it's such a powerful question. I've been thinking about that for a while. Here are three possible ways to deal with it. But I don't find any of them fully satisfying at this point, so this is the nightmare question for me, the thing I keep thinking about.

Immerwahr's response to this job candidate's open admission of not having fully resolved a significant element of the project? "Hire that guy. Hire him so hard. He turned the worst moment into the best moment because we saw him listening, thinking, reacting. We weren't trying to get a bulletproof talk. We were trying to get a scholar, and that's what he showed he was."

What if a questioner is rude? This doesn't happen often, but it happens. Keep in mind that in academia, it is not rude for people to ask challenging questions in a confrontational, even brusque or harsh manner. Arguing is an academic's love language, and tough questions demonstrate that questioners are interested in your ideas, respect your ability to defend them, and are giving you a chance to show how sharp you are. You should be much more worried if all your questions are easy ones. That can be a sign that people didn't like the talk and are being gentle out of pity. Critical, polemical, and even antagonistic questions usually mean that the questioner is giving you a chance to show your chops while simultaneously displaying theirs. If you're giving a job talk, some questioners may already be anticipating advocating for you at the hiring meeting and will ask tough questions to bolster the case they want to make for you later.

Know yourself. If you've been drawn to academia because you love disputation, you'll feel energized by tough questions asked toughly and will automatically answer enthusiastically, without defensiveness. Many academics love arguing so much that they don't hear hostility even when it's there. We should all aim to occupy that headspace. It's also the case that some people who love doing research don't love having people challenge every element of their painstaking work. If you're one of those people, tell your test audience to go to town during your practice Q&A so that you can rehearse answering intense questions. It used to be that graduate students had many opportunities to practice being grilled because it was common for professors to conduct qualifying examinations and dissertation defenses like inquisitions. These days, faculty often adopt a mellow tone even when asking tough questions. I think that's a good thing. But it means that younger scholars don't have many occasions to respond to questions posed in a challenging, even aggressive manner.

In the rare case that an audience member is unusually antagonistic or condescending or misrepresents what you said, the best way to assert yourself is to be a better person than they are. As David Levine put it, if someone is being hostile, "you wrong-foot them by being open and available." Robert Mawhinney made a similar point. If asked a question rudely, don't be shocked or reactive. De-escalate by gently asking them to clarify. If someone asks a pointed question in what sounds to you like a dismissive or patronizing tone, disarm them by politely asking them to rephrase it: "I'm not clear exactly about what you're asking; can you rephrase the question?" Odds are good that the second time, they will tone things down. Even if they don't, you should always, as Branden Joseph put it, "answer the question in its most generous form."

Answer questions in the most generous form even when the question contains a factual error. Joseph described giving a talk on the artist Robert Rauschenberg where someone asked him why he hadn't talked about the artist's Jewishness. The answer was simple: Rauschenberg isn't Jewish. But Joseph didn't begin his answer by flatly contradicting the questioner. Instead, he responded by discussing Rauschenberg's relationship to religion, which enabled him to clear up the misunderstanding without embarrassing his interlocutor. This illustrates Robert Mawhinney's basic principle for how to conduct a Q&A: it's a conversation, not a contest, and in a conversation, you work *with* the other person.

Sometimes an audience member is so overbearing and condescending that you have to push back a tiny bit. A questioner may imply or state outright that your work is not theoretically sophisticated enough or that your findings are insufficiently bold. This can happen to any speaker, but it tends to follow predictable patterns related to how people perceive status and attribute competence, so people of color and people perceived to be feminine usually experience more of this. If you're in one of these groups, you are unfortunately likely to have encountered this long before you start giving talks and will have found strategies for addressing these situations by consulting mentors, colleagues, and friends.

Most of the experts I interviewed concurred that the speaker will gain the upper hand by being calmer and more polite than a needling or rude questioner. They also agreed that it is okay, when responding to a question that undermines your authority, to repeat what makes your research methods sound and your findings original or accurate. "You raise an interesting question about X, and if we had found any evidence of X, it would indeed mean Y. But in our eight experiments involving a total of two thousand subjects, we never encountered evidence of X." And if someone is really out of hand and making you uncomfortable, don't shy away from confronting them directly. Michèle Lamont put this best: "Don't be afraid to be a bit of a badass" when fielding questions, even if you're more junior than the people asking them.

How to Ask Questions Effectively

Many of the expert speakers I interviewed mentioned that as graduate students, they first prepared to give talks by pushing themselves to ask a question at every lecture they attended. English professor Rebecca Walkowitz tells graduate advisees that their job when attending talks is to formulate a question, even if they don't ask it. Audience members at all career stages should try to come up with a question—it's the collegial thing to do.

There is an art to asking good questions, just as there is an art to giving good talks. Since the aim of this book is to improve academic talks in general, this section ends with some thoughts about posing questions effectively.

I recommend opening your question by stating your name, status, and departmental affiliation. "Hi, I'm Sharon Marcus, a professor in the English Department." This is rarely done, but it's helpful and gracious. People like to know who they're talking to, and this information can also help contextualize your question for everyone in the room.

If your question includes an acronym, explain what it stands for. I once saw someone ask a question about "HSBC" that took a while for the speaker to get because it can be difficult to hear names accurately, especially abbreviated ones. If the questioner had said "HSBC Bank," things would have gone more smoothly.

Just as a speaker should avoid saying, "Thanks for that great question," I think it's borderline condescending for questioners to offer assessments, even when couched as appreciation. It's very common for audience members to say things like, "Thanks for that interesting talk," or worse, "That was a nice look at X." Statements like these often sound patronizing even when that wasn't the intention. If you feel compelled to express your appreciation of the talk before posing your question, I recommend making your assessment substantive by being specific about what you learned: "I found your discussion of X very informative because I was not aware of Y."

Don't apologize for your question: "That was my question, I apologize for its bad formulation." Either ask a question in a way that doesn't require saying you're sorry or give yourself a break; people admire elegantly phrased questions, but they don't expect them.

Do not repeat what the speaker argued back to them as though you're the one making their point or making their point better than they did. I've seen this happen a lot, and it doesn't reflect well on the echoer. Here's how I saw one speaker handle this. After an audience member recited back to her what she had just said, in one of those "this is more of a comment than a question" moves, she responded: "That is a very nice rearticulation of the point I'm trying to make." To my mind, that was more generous than the echoer deserved, because she had made her point very clearly, which was precisely why the questioner could parrot it back to her so readily. Nonetheless, her reply did adhere to the tenet that one should respond to the question in its most generous form and disarm rude people by being gentle and gracious.

A good question, Rebecca Walkowitz noted, begins with listening carefully during the talk. One easy thing to listen for is how to relate the speaker's key ideas to something in your area of expertise. Note that this is different from asking, "How does this apply to my area of expertise?" Instead, you are asking, "If I transfer this idea to another area that I know about, *which is related to your area in the following way*, how would it work there?" Good academic ideas are portable, and good academic questions help the speaker see how their ideas might translate into a different setting. As Walkowitz put it, "My job is to come up with a question that helps me understand better what the speaker did and helps me think about how that is usable beyond the space already discussed."

If you paid close attention to the talk and didn't understand something, it is perfectly acceptable to ask about that: "I didn't get this one particular move, can you help me understand it better?" Most of the time, if you didn't get something, others didn't get it either. They'll be grateful you asked and admire you for being confident enough to admit that something confused you. If you didn't fully understand how the speaker answered a previous question, and it relates to one you have, you can say something like, "I think you just answered my question, but I'm going to ask it anyway to make sure I got it right." This acknowledges that your query might be redundant and makes clear that your motivation is to understand the talk as well as possible.

Many academic audience members ask highly specialized questions. Academics further from the speaker's subfield may ask more general questions. As an audience member, you can fall back on the following questions, and as a speaker, you can practice answering some of these when doing advance prep for the Q&A.

- What was your motivation for this project?
- What surprised you most while doing this research?
- How would your argument change if you included [insert example speaker did not discuss]?
- What would happen to your argument if you scaled it up or down?
- What do you find people most often misconstrue about your claims?

It can be scary to field questions. But if you know the material in your talk well, have pruned some interesting points, and practice answering common types of questions, you can anticipate and prepare for much of what your audience will ask.

Since one key purpose of giving academic talks is to help you improve work in progress, tough questions should spark joy. People ask tough questions to show that they're engaged, that they respect your intelligence, and that they're smart, too.

You don't have to answer every question authoritatively in the moment. Acknowledge what you don't know, and pivot to what you do. Your job is not to prove that you have all the answers but to model how you would go about finding them and that you understand how and why questions that you can't answer matter.

Answer questions graciously and generously, even when the questioner is being curmudgeonly or you can't answer fully, and you'll convince everyone of your intellectual and collegial merits. Answer questions sincerely, by welcoming feedback during your talk and outlining how you'd tackle the issues raised when revising your material for publication, and both you and your work will be the better for it.

6

Slides

"ONE QUESTION I have for you is about slides . . . they can be a real problem."

The expert voicing this skepticism about multimedia presentations in academic talks was David Levine, a professor of theater, dance, and media. When we spoke, he was busy preparing an installation at the Museum of the Moving Image that involved a talking, volumetric hologram, so he's far from being a Luddite. And as a professional theater director, Levine never objects to putting on a show.

What Levine does object to is putting on a bad show. And he and I agree: slides in academic talks are often not a good scene.

This chapter will explain when to use slides and how to design them more effectively. I will argue, backed by scientific research, that

- **Only a handful of situations in academic talks *require* slides.**
- **Speakers should almost never put more than a few words on a slide and should almost never read aloud the words on a slide verbatim.**

- **There are scientifically proven ways to design and present slides effectively, and academic speakers should use them.**

For those of you who think you already know the best practices for slide design and presentation: spoiler alert. The best practices I'll be presenting here go beyond basics such as facing your audience while talking through a slide and using fonts large enough to be legible in the back of the room. And even those basics will bear repeating, because many people don't follow them.

And now, a brief polemic.

Scientific studies show that most of the slides people use in talks are at best inessential and at worst detrimental to learning.

Before presenting you with the science, here is some anecdotal evidence that slides are not essential. Early in my research, I watched a video recording of a talk in which the camera had captured the speaker but not their slides. After some initial frustration, I started to notice that it didn't matter at all: I could follow the talk by just listening to it.

After that, I began to conduct an informal experiment—one that you can replicate. Sometimes, when accessing talks via YouTube, I would shift about halfway through the recording from watching and listening to just listening. Occasionally I went into audio-only mode after the first thirty seconds.

Every single time, I could follow the talk without seeing the slides at all.

This held true for talks in all disciplines, including ones far from my areas of expertise. It even held true for talks involving charts, graphs, film clips, and images of artworks, because speakers followed the best practice of describing what they were showing. To be sure, in cases involving data visualizations and visual or audiovisual art, I learned more when I could see the material. I'm not advocating that we all attend talks wearing blindfolds or that speakers stop using slides altogether. If the norms in your discipline require slides, you have to use them. But keep in mind that poorly designed slides make talks *harder* to follow than no slides at all.

The bulk of this chapter will explain how to make your slides better. But before I do that, what can we learn from my experience of being able to follow good academic talks just by listening to them? I'll answer that question via an analogy between academic talks and a far more popular genre for presenting information and arguments: the podcast.

A good talk resembles a good podcast, and podcasts are designed to work well without visuals.

Podcasts prove that you don't need a "multimedia circus" (Levine's term) to hold your audience's attention or convince them of your claims. All you need is a good script, delivered well. *You* deliver that script, not your slides (see chapter 7). Indeed, I'd speculate that evading the difficulties of developing a good script and delivering it well explains why academics, so many of us shy introverts, love showing slides. Used as prompts, slides help us avoid the indispensable but laborious process of internalizing our script (see chapter 8). Used as armor, slides screen the speaker from being the focus of attention by giving the audience something else to look at.[1]

1. Jacqueline Gartner-Schmidt, a speech pathologist and author of an article on public speaking in the age of hybrid and virtual presentations, observes that in

You may protest, as some I've talked to have, that slides can help many audience members focus and understand the talk better. Maybe my ability to do without visual materials is just my own cognitive quirk.

That's not what the science says, though. There's a lot of research on PowerPoint presentations in the lecture classroom. Most of it demonstrates that slides either have no effect on learning or obstruct it.[2] Academic talks have some important differences from course lectures, but both formats involve sharing knowledge through words delivered in person, so the research on undergraduate courses is relevant for academic talks. Indeed, one set of researchers conducting a meta-analysis of forty-eight studies of PowerPoint effectiveness found that, when they disaggregated studies of K–12 students from studies of college students and scientific conferences, **the more informed the audience, the less useful slides were.**[3]

---

practice, the main purpose of slides is to "script and shield" the presenter, not to engage the audience. Jacqueline Gartner-Schmidt, "The New Normal—Virtual and Hybrid Presentations: Developing Content, Designing Slides, and Delivery Guidelines," *Ear, Nose & Throat Journal* 101, no. 9S (2022): 21S. See also Mann and Robinson, "Boredom in the Lecture Theatre," 246.

2. James P. Baker, Alan K. Goodboy, Nicholas D. Bowman, and Alyssa A. Wright, "Does Teaching with PowerPoint Increase Students' Learning? A Meta-analysis," *Computers & Education* 126 (2018): 377; the studies cited in Mann and Robinson, "Boredom in the Lecture Theatre," 245; and Debra L. Worthington and David G. Levasseur, "To Provide or Not to Provide Course PowerPoint Slides? The Impact of Instructor-Provided Slides upon Student Attendance and Performance," *Computers & Education* 85 (2015): 15.

3. Baker et al., "Does Teaching with PowerPoint Increase Students' Learning?," 379.

Many students prefer lectures with slides and are convinced that slides help them learn better. They say so in their course evaluations, and they say so when polled by learning scientists. This proves that students *think* they are learning better with slides, but there's also significant evidence that students are wrong to think this. When scientists objectively measure how well students are learning, they find that PowerPoint either has no effect at all or "has strong drawbacks."[4] This holds true whether scientists measure learning through grades, through simple tests of recall, or through open-ended essay questions. Some researchers have tested whether students learn better without slides.[5] A particularly telling experiment studied 204 students enrolled in a large lecture course on communication theory across two semesters. The students were exposed to identical lecture material, delivered in three different ways. One set of students saw slides along with classroom lectures. A second set had optional access to slides. A third set had no access to slides at all. The students

4. Mohamed Kara-Mohamed, "Teaching Without PowerPoint Slides in Engineering: A Pilot Study," *International Journal of Mechanical Engineering Education* 53 (2024): 12.

5. A meta-analysis of forty-eight studies of PowerPoint in the classroom reveals that, when lecture material remains the same, the presence or absence of slides has no effect on student learning; Baker et al., "Does Teaching with PowerPoint Increase Students' Learning?," 376. This finding may be specific to PowerPoint slides rather than visual aids in general (e.g., blackboards, whiteboards, overhead transparencies); Mann and Robinson cite a study in which students performed worse when a professor switched from overhead transparencies to PowerPoint slides ("Boredom in the Lecture Theatre," 245).

who did best were the ones with zero slide exposure. Any use of slides had "an adverse impact on course performance."[6]

Students are experts on what they like, but they are not experts on what helps them learn effectively. The same may be true of academics.[7]

Given that most slides are either useless or harmful, I advise against asking yourself, "*Can* I turn this into a slide?" Just because you can doesn't mean that you should. Nor is the right question "Is this slide relevant?" Research shows that academic lecturers are terrible judges of relevance. Audience members often find images that speakers consider obviously relevant either confusing or at odds with the points they are meant to illustrate.[8]

I recommend asking yourself this: **"What can a slide or clip convey here that words alone cannot?"** There can be many good answers to this question. Your slide or clip may be sharing evidence that is itself visual or multimedia. Your slide may add important knowledge or context to your words. Your slide may visualize data and information far more compactly than words alone could. Those are great reasons to include slides. Share those reasons with your audience by making them explicit in your talk. As Mariana Alessandri put it in our inter-

6. Worthington and Levasseur, "To Provide or Not to Provide Course PowerPoint Slides?," 14.

7. As Baker et al. note, "Students tend to self-report more learning from PowerPoint instruction than what performance-based measures reflect" ("Does Teaching with PowerPoint Increase Students' Learning?," 379).

8. Joanna Wolfe, Nisha Shanmugaraj, Juliann Reineke, Laura Caton Peet, and Craig P. Moreau, "Advancing the Knowledge Base on Effective Presentation Slide Design: Three Pilot Studies," *Journal of Technical Writing and Communication* 54, no. 3 (2024): 252.

view, when you show your audience a slide, always tell them why it's there. Elisheva Baumgarten did this in her talk on Jews, Christians, and medieval prayer when she showed an image from a Jewish text, described it, and explained how it demonstrated that medieval European Jews felt comfortable in urban settings that were majority Christian (Figure 4). Baumgarten did what all academic speakers should do each and every time we show a slide: she told us (a) what we were seeing, (b) the important point the slide made, and (c) how it made it.[9]

Some readers will have a presenter-focused objection at this point: "I use slides to remind myself of my talk's outline. How will I remember what I need to say without putting my outline on my slides?" I have three responses to this. First, good academic talks prioritize the audience, not the speaker. Second, if you strongly prefer to be prompted by slides, you need to prompt yourself with slides that foreground visual evidence plus a headline (more on that below). Third, if you need your prompts to be more detailed than headlines (I would), you will have to separate your prompts from your slides. Your prompts do not have to be on a screen. You can print your outline, script, and notes or write them out on sheets of paper or on index cards before your talk and then hold them in your hand or place them on a podium while delivering your talk, which will also free your body from being tethered to a screen. Chapters 7 and 8 will offer more guidance

9. Elisheva Baumgarten, "Shared Appeals to Different Gods: Jews, Christians and Medieval Prayer," Helen Diller Distinguished Annual Lecture, Center for Jewish Studies, University of California, Berkeley, February 21, 2023, posted March 11, 2023, by @Berkeley Center for Jewish Studies, YouTube video, 1:19:48, https://www.youtube.com/watch?v=904TwPbA7b0.

FIGURE 4. Slide from a talk by Elisheva Baumgarten, "Shared Appeals to Different Gods: Jews, Christians and Medieval Prayer," February 21, 2023. Image used with the permission of Elisheva Baumgarten.

about how to work with physical prompts. The bottom line: Only you are giving your talk, and only you need to see your cue cards.

When and How to Use Slides

Let's turn to specific situations that require slides or audiovisual (AV) material. All involve evidence that must be seen or heard or that can be presented more efficiently and vividly if you show as well as tell.[10]

10. TED talks are known for being visually snazzy, but even Chris Anderson's guide to delivering these recommends using visuals "to show something that's hard to describe" or explain (*TED Talks*, 114–15).

Use slides to present data and data visualizations that you discuss in depth. Strictly speaking, data means facts gathered for reference and analysis. In this sense, literary passages, images of artworks, and maps are all data. Colloquially, however, academics usually apply the term *data* to quantitative evidence—findings that can be expressed as numbers, statistics, or equations, often compressed into charts or graphs. As Robert Mawhinney put it in our interview, the main purpose of slides in the sciences is the compact presentation of complex data. Scientists, like art historians, were early adopters of slides and plastic transparencies. As some of the first academics to use computers, scientists also were early inventors and users of software for visual presentations.

Always begin by telling the audience what your slide shows, then explain how it relates to your claims. Many speakers do not do this. Some put up color-coded charts and never explain what the colors mean. Others show graphs whose x- and y-axes are either unlabeled or labeled in illegibly small type. Some put up complex slides, say nothing about them, and don't keep them on the screen long enough for the audience to puzzle them out on their own.

Never assume that you can forgo verbalizing a point because it is on a slide and the audience can read it for themselves. As Mawhinney modeled in our interview, start with the basics: "This star has a mass of 10." Then explain why that matters: "That's really noticeable, because we didn't expect to find something that massive in this location." Do the same when explaining graphs and charts. Begin by stating, "The x-axis represents this; the y-axis represents that." Then shift to how the chart relates to your key claim: "There's an interesting phenomenon here, where there's a wiggle in the curve, which means that. . . ." For a series of great explanations of visual materials, I recommend watching Rotem Sorek's talk on immune systems in bacteria, in which he deployed a series of phrases that any academic lecturer showing slides should keep in their rhetorical tool kit: "What you see here is . . . ," "The reason I'm showing you this is. . . ."[11]

Use slides to present visual or multimedia evidence that you will analyze in depth or that makes your topic come alive for the audience. In many disciplines, visual and multimedia materials *are* the evidence. If the topic is a newly detected galaxy, a potential vaccine against a particular type of cancer cell, Euler-Lagrange equations, data about how recessions impact voting patterns, Renaissance sculpture, Beethoven's symphonies, film noir, the current state of rainforests, or the history of kitchen implements, the audience needs to be able to see or hear representations of key examples in order to understand what the speaker is saying and decide for themselves whether they agree.

Slides and clips can also be compact, vivid ways to bring the audience into the world of your talk. Historian Brodwyn Fischer did this in a talk about Brazilian history where she contrasted the manicured image of the port city of Recife presented on nineteenth-century postcards to the more complex picture offered by historical documents located in a Recife

11. Rotem Sorek, "The Immune System of Bacteria: Beyond CRISPR," NIH Director's Wednesday Afternoon Lecture Series, National Institutes of Health, January 25, 2023, posted January 30, 2023, by @NIH VideoCast, YouTube video, 1:03:07, https://www.youtube.com/watch?v=_COeBSfG53g.

archive (see Figure 5). Immediately after mentioning that archive, Fischer announced, "And that's where I'd like to take you now," shifting to a photograph of Recife's Memorial da Justiça, where she had found many of the materials on which her talk was based.[12]

Whether presenting audiovisual materials as evidence or to provide vivid context, the advice that Branden Joseph told me he gives to graduate students holds true for all disciplines, including the sciences and social sciences: "Don't take for granted that people see your visual materials the way you see them." Always begin by describing what you see and, if using materials that include sound, what you hear. Focus especially on what might not be obvious to those who, unlike you, are not experts. (As discussed in chapter 8, your test audiences can help you determine what is and isn't obvious to nonexperts.) Art historians excel at providing rich analytical descriptions of their materials. If you want a great example of how to do this, I recommend watching Joseph Koerner's talk on Albrecht Dürer, which began with an amazing breakdown of a 1520 sketch Dürer did of Antwerp's harbor. Koerner pointed out where the sketch is more and less precise, drew our attention to the interplay between crowded and empty space, identified the point at the center where the image's lone

12. Brodwyn Fischer, "Intimate Inequalities," Radcliffe Institute for Advanced Study at Harvard University, September 26, 2022, posted March 31, 2023, by @Harvard Radcliffe Institute, YouTube video, 59:51, https://www.youtube.com/watch?v=0TGMm6LASrU.

FIGURE 5. Screenshot from a talk by Brodwyn Fischer, "Intimate Inequalities," September 26, 2022. (The words at the bottom of the image that misspell the archive's name were generated by the Zoom transcription.) Image used with the permission of Brodwyn Fischer and the Radcliffe Institute for Advanced Study at Harvard University.

human figures appear, and then connected all those details to the talk's topic: Dürer's mobility.[13]

For an artwork, nonobvious features include the work's actual size, the materials used to make it, when it was made, and small but telling details that will feature in your argument. If you put up a slide of the medieval "Unicorn Rests in a Garden" tapestry (Figure 6), you can start by saying: Here is a medieval tapestry, the "Unicorn Rests in a Garden," currently held in the Cloisters museum in New York City. We still don't know exactly who manufactured it, but experts have

13. Joseph Koerner, "Dürer's Mobility," 2021 Linbury Lecture, National Gallery, January 14, 2022, posted March 7, 2022, by @The National Gallery, YouTube video, 1:34:52, https://www.youtube.com/watch?v=FqsCni1i9AY.

determined that it was probably made in the Netherlands in the late fifteenth century, using silk, wool, and metallic thread. It measures about 145 by 99 inches. At its center you see a unicorn with red marks on its white fur. Scholars agree that these red marks do not represent blood but are meant to depict juice dripping onto the unicorn from the pomegranates hanging in the tree above it. The tapestry is famous for depicting roughly a hundred different kinds of flowers, but I'd also like to draw your attention to the small dragonfly depicted in the center of the image, just underneath and a bit to the right of the unicorn's back hooves. Only a few scholars have discussed this dragonfly at all, and they have argued that the dragonfly symbolizes X. By contrast, I will be arguing that the dragonfly symbolizes Y.

This two-part protocol—tell your audience *what* they are seeing and *why* you are showing it to them—may seem obvious, but I can't stress enough that most speakers don't follow it. Instead, they show things on slides because they can, because they think they are cool, or because they feel obligated to show slides. All of these motivations produce slides that make talks less good. Sure, if you're talking about a historical figure from eighteenth-century Britain, it might be useful to show a portrait of him. But I think it's distracting and confusing and a waste of your audience's limited attention to show a portrait of that figure and then say *absolutely nothing* about it (which, like every example I discuss in this book, is not my hypothetical invention but something I witnessed firsthand). Show that portrait only if it explains something that we wouldn't otherwise understand. No one wants to look at a mediocre painting of some eighteenth-century dude in a

FIGURE 6. "The Unicorn Rests in a Garden," ca. 1495–1505. Image donated to Wikimedia Commons by the Metropolitan Museum of Art.

white wig and red jacket for its own sake. And if we did, that wouldn't be good for the talk, either, because we'd be focusing on the dude's white wig and red jacket while the speaker discusses something else entirely.

People who study effective teaching and communication have a phrase for tempting examples that speakers include simply because they seem interesting, evocative, or cool: "seductive details."[14] Those seductive details are competing with you for the audience's attention, and they are winning.

A couple of the experts I interviewed mentioned that sometimes they show slides that have only an oblique, atmospheric relationship to their material. They argued, eloquently, that audiences now expect slides and that evocative slides can, like wallpaper or a film soundtrack, help establish a mood. Just as a podcast periodically underscores words with music, some scholars use images to counterpoint their words. I'm sure this works well for the experts I spoke with, because everything they do, they do well. Their approach may be harder for the rest of us mere mortals to pull off, especially if we are pressed for time. If you insist on going this route, make sure to conduct a dress rehearsal and ask for feedback about any atmospheric visuals: Did those slides add something important to the talk, and if so, what?

14. Ruth Garner, Mark G. Gillingham, and C. Stephen White first coined this term to refer to distracting textual details; see their "Effects of 'Seductive Details' on Macroprocessing and Microprocessing in Adults and Children," *Cognition and Instruction* 6, no. 1 (1989): 41–57. Shannon F. Harp and Richard Mayer extend that finding to include distractingly pleasing visuals in "How Seductive Details Do Their Damage: A Theory of Cognitive Interest in Science Learning," *Journal of Educational Psychology* 90, no. 3 (1996): 414–34.

Another reason to use slides only when necessary: a speaker's presenting capacity is almost unlimited, but an audience's processing capacity is very constrained. You, with your limitless presenting capacity, can show slides, play music, release balloons, hand out candy, and periodically spritz the room with perfume and still do a decent job presenting your script. But just because you can doesn't mean that you should. Audience attention is limited. Do not squander it. As Jacqueline Gartner-Schmidt puts it, "A slide represents valuable real estate—use it wisely."[15] If an image or clip does not prove a crucial point better than words alone could, it is a seductive detail. Eliminate it.

The one exception to the rule of only showing slides that you analyze in depth is a big one, but it is also not really an exception. As I explain in chapter 10, when presenting on Zoom, it is often best to minimize the view the audience has of you as speaker so that you are just a small box in a corner or side of the screen. If you have to fill the screen with images for the entirety of your talk, some of them won't be essential to your argument. But all those images will still be doing something that your words alone (on Zoom) cannot: filling the audience's screen with something more engaging than a very large close-up of you looking down or to the side as you consult your notes.

What are some other examples of essential slides? Speakers often need slides or handouts **to present *textual* evidence that will be analyzed in depth**. Weaving quotations from sources into one's own prose is a key technique of scholarly

15. Gartner-Schmidt, "New Normal," 22S.

writing, whether one is analyzing a novel, citing important theorists, narrating a historical event, or doing ethnography. As I noted in chapter 2, mixing other people's words with your own can be challenging when delivering a talk. In print, we have many ways to distinguish what we are saying from what we are citing: quotation marks, block quotes, parenthetical citations, footnotes, and even italics. In speech, however, we have to signal verbally where quotes begin and end, in ways that can be awkward, laborious, and hard to follow. That's why chapter 2 recommended that academic speakers foreground their own voices, paraphrase liberally, and quote sources verbatim less frequently than published versions of the same material might.

Sometimes, however, a long quotation is a key piece of evidence that receives extended analysis. The most common instance of this is in literary studies, where talks frequently involve closely reading passages from poems or novels, although scholars in other fields do this as well. Literary close reading involves dissecting a passage's formal qualities—syntax, rhythm, meter, word choice, word sounds, and figures of speech—and interpreting how those reinforce or complicate the passage's content. Like any dissection, a close reading should be thorough. An eminent literary critic once told me that his rule of thumb for doing a truly close reading was to make sure that his commentary on a passage took up at least twice as much space as the passage itself. I was a bit surprised that a scholar renowned for his sophistication used such a blunt, empirical measure, but in the years since he shared that with me, I've tried it, and it does offer an excellent test of whether a close reading is truly close. If you're not taking twice as much time to talk about your passage as you do to read it aloud, either say more about it or shorten your quote.

If you are reading a passage closely enough to merit placing it on a slide, then your audience needs to see it to follow your claims about it and determine whether they agree with them. In the olden days, people put these passages on paper handouts, which had the advantage of limiting the number of passages included to what could fit on a page. Of the sixty talks in my corpus, only one included a physical handout—a talk by Kathryn Lofton, professor of religion at Yale University.[16] Handouts have some advantages over slides if all they contain are block quotes. Unlike AV presentations, printouts are not subject to last-minute tech snafus. Paper handouts don't require you to speak in the dark or talk over a noisy projector fan. People can bring handouts as close to their eyes as needed, mark them up, refer to them during the Q&A, and take them home as a souvenir.

I'm guessing, though, that most readers of this book will want to put the passages they read closely on slides. If you do that, make sure to format the quotes in a font large enough to be legible to people at the back of the room and consider following the suggestions I offer later in this chapter about when to read passages aloud versus when to show them to your audience.

Use slides to present names, foreign words, technical terms, and other unfamiliar terms. In my early years as a

16. Kathryn Lofton, "Sensitive People: On Being Alive Today," Institute for Religion, Culture and Public Life, Columbia University, September 18, 2023.

professor, I had the good fortune to co-teach a course with a brilliant classicist, Leslie Kurke. Before each lecture, she went to the blackboard and wrote out names and terms that an undergraduate might not already know. If you've never heard of Euripides or Alcibiades, anagnorisis or agape, you'd be hard-pressed to know how to spell those words or even how to aurally process them the first time you heard them. It was a canny and considerate pedagogical practice, one that I use to this day.

When giving an academic lecture, you won't always have access to a blackboard, and you should honor your academic audience's desire to be treated as possessing expertise. If I'm giving a talk in an English literature department, I can and should assume that most people present know who Pierre Bourdieu is and have probably heard his name pronounced properly. But it's also a safe guess that some people present won't know who he is or may have seen his name but don't know how it's pronounced. Slides can help here. They are a good resource for visually presenting *essential* terms that you have reason to believe some people in your audience may have difficulty processing through hearing alone.

Similarly, if you're using an unusual phrase or a term in a language most of your audience doesn't know well, put the unusual term on a slide and show that slide the first time you use the term. Barbara Henry did this in her talk on the underworld in Russian literature when she put the term "katabasis" on a slide and defined it as the Greek term for "descent" or "the way down." By contrast, as a Slavicist speaking to other Slavicists, she rarely spelled Russian names out. This was understandable, but as a nonspecialist interested in her topic, I could have used help with those.[17] I once heard a talk in which the speaker used a Latin phrase to name one of his key concepts. The audience did not consist primarily of classicists, and even if it had, some scholars who don't know Latin might have been present. I had no idea what he was saying, let alone what the term meant, until he happened to put up a slide that included the mystery locution.

When you put a key term on a slide, don't include a definition. Just show the term. (Or, in the Bourdieu example, show some of his book covers.) As I advise below, slides should never contain long strings of text that you then paraphrase or read aloud verbatim. If a slide with only one or two words on it feels too bare, add an image that, in adherence to the rule above, explains the term in a way that goes beyond what words alone can do. For example, when giving a talk about a figure in Serbian folklore to a group of mostly anglophone scholars, you might show a slide that spells out the folkloric figure's name in Serbian and shows an image of the figure. While showing the slide, explain how the image you've selected to illustrate one of your talk's key terms underscores your claims about it.

In addition to being an effective way to share unfamiliar terms with your audience, slides can also convey information

17. Barbara Henry, "Road, River, and Book: The Russian Literary Underworld," Sawchen Lecture Series in Slavic Studies, Department of Central, Eastern, and Northern European Studies, University of British Columbia, and Bicentennial Speaker Series, 2020–21, North American Dostoevsky Society, January 26, 2021, posted March 19, 2021, by @North American Dostoevsky Society, YouTube video, 54:09, https://www.youtube.com/watch?v=utjsnbRq2HM.

it would be inappropriate or time-consuming to read aloud. Here are three examples of that:

- **Use slides to identify yourself.** If you are using slides, consider creating an introductory slide that people see when they first enter the room, before your talk begins. That slide can include your name, affiliation, and email address, along with the title, date, and place of your talk. This slide can also feature an image that you will discuss later in the talk, but keep it small so that you have room to present all the words on the slide in a font large enough to be visible even at the back of the room. If you're not showing slides at all, you can skip this one.
- **Use slides to credit collaborators.** Much scientific research involves dozens of people whom speakers don't have time to name one by one. Instead, they show photographs of individual collaborators when discussing their findings, as well as group photos of their entire team, labeled with names.
- **Use slides to present sources and references in bulk.** Often people use slides to provide a compact literature review. An effective way to do this that doesn't involve putting lots of words on slides is to create slides showing the covers of several books crucial to the project.

Even when your slides contain very few words, **never read aloud what you put on a slide**. This is one of the most common things speakers do with slides: put words on them and then proceed to read those words aloud verbatim. Also fairly common, and even more inimical to giving a good talk: putting up a lengthy passage and then telling people that you *won't* be reading it or discussing it but that they can read it for themselves. You will be shocked, shocked, shocked, to hear that I think these are both terrible practices if you want people to hear and take in what you have to say. As Harvard sociology professor Michèle Lamont observed during our interview, "People cannot read the slide and listen to you at the same time."

When giving a talk you have one job: to help people listen to you. Don't show slides that encourage your audience to tune you out. You wouldn't play a recording of a famous speech and simultaneously read a transcript of that speech aloud at a different pace from the speaker on the recording. That's basically what you're doing when you put words on a slide and read them aloud while your audience tries to read the same words to themselves. As one expert puts it, "Words on the screen are fighting your presentation, not enhancing it."[18] As another notes, once you put more than a few words on a slide, you have "rendered yourself, the presenter, useless, because people will read your slides versus listen to you."[19] One of the most widely cited peer-reviewed articles on effective presentations agrees: "Avoid presenting identical streams of printed and spoken words."[20]

18. Anderson, *TED Talks*, 117.

19. Gartner-Schmidt, "New Normal," 22S.

20. Richard E. Mayer and Roxana Moreno, "Nine Ways to Reduce Cognitive Load in Multimedia Learning," *Educational Psychologist* 38, no. 1 (2003): 46. Rebecca Walkowitz made the same point in our interview, listing as one of her pet peeves the tendency to put most of a talk on slides and then read aloud what the audience can and will read to themselves, which leaves her thinking, "Just send me the slides and give me back my hour."

Some people reading this will want a more detailed explanation about why people cannot read your slides and listen to you at the same time, so here it is. We read faster than we speak, so audiences read the words on slides to themselves faster than you can recite them.[21] Furthermore, we process printed words on a screen in two ways: as sounds, in the auditory channel, and as images, in the visual channel. Each channel has a limited capacity for holding and processing information. Listening to someone say words while we read them creates cognitive overload.[22] We combat that overload to our verbal and visual channels by shutting down one of the overloaded channels.[23]

This is why learning experts advise speakers to keep words exclusively in the verbal/auditory channel.[24] In other words, do not show people your long quotations; read them aloud. *You* need to see the text as you read it aloud. The audience does not. During a talk, the best way for listeners to process words is to hear them, not see them.

"But how is my audience going to understand my chart if I don't add a lot of text explaining it?" They are going to understand your chart because you are going to talk them through it. They will listen to your explanation of the chart more attentively, *and* look at your chart more closely, if you

21. Gartner-Schmidt, "New Normal," 22S.

22. Mayer and Moreno, "Nine Ways to Reduce Cognitive Load in Multimedia Learning," 43.

23. Wolfe et al., "Advancing the Knowledge Base on Effective Presentation Slide Design," 237, 253.

24. See Mayer and Moreno, "Nine Ways to Reduce Cognitive Load in Multimedia Learning."

do not distract them with a bunch of text. "But how is my audience going to process my long quotations if they can't see them?" They are going to process your quotations by listening to you read them, and they will process them better if you present those quotations through one channel and one channel only: the verbal, auditory one that makes a talk a talk. If your test audiences tell you that a particular quote was too long to follow when you read it aloud, then trim or paraphrase that quote.

There's one special case that requires further discussion: close readings of long passages. As I said above, close readings *do* require that you show the audience the passages—but not right away. Here's how to avoid overloading your audience when doing close readings. Start by reading the passage aloud to your audience, verbatim, without yet showing it and without yet offering any analysis or commentary. Having read the passage aloud once, then, and only then, put up a slide displaying it. Now launch into your close reading, using a pointer, annotation tools, or animations to highlight individual elements as you interpret them. Do something similar with close analysis of musical compositions or with clips from theater, dance, or film. Start by stating your key claims about a clip and then identify a few things the audience should look and listen for as they watch it for the first time. After playing it once, comment on it some more, then play it again, pausing to single out what you just explained: "This is the key change I was talking about, which proves X" or "Right here is the dissolve I mentioned, which I'm arguing does Y."

If you are an anthropologist, sociologist, or political scientist quoting an interview subject at length, and you have permission to do this, I recommend that you start by playing a recording of the subject speaking. When I've heard speakers do this, the audience was riveted. If you're a historian analyzing a speech delivered in the last hundred years or so, it's similarly evocative to play or show a clip of the original speech. Show quotations from the speech only after playing the recording—and only if you are analyzing their language in detail.

Some of you may be wondering whether you can really forgo the road maps, bullet-point lists, and summaries that constitute the majority of many academic speakers' slides. By now, you can anticipate what I'm going to say. Audiences do not need to see your main points written out on a slide. They need to hear them from you. Slides should emphasize images, not words. "Slides are supplementary, not primary. . . . The message the talk is intended to convey comes from you, not from the slide. So, tell them verbally; do not write it all out on your slides."[25] For this reason, I don't think it's necessary to include slides that say "Introduction," list section titles, or provide overviews of the talk's key moves. If you do, keep your section titles simple. Each time you transition to a new section, show the road map slide again, highlighting the title of the section you are about to begin. Figure 7 shows an example of this from early in Elisheva Baumgarten's talk. If you're pressed for time and need to choose between working on what you will say and creating slides, spend your time on the

25. Friman, "Behavior Analysts to the Front!," 116.

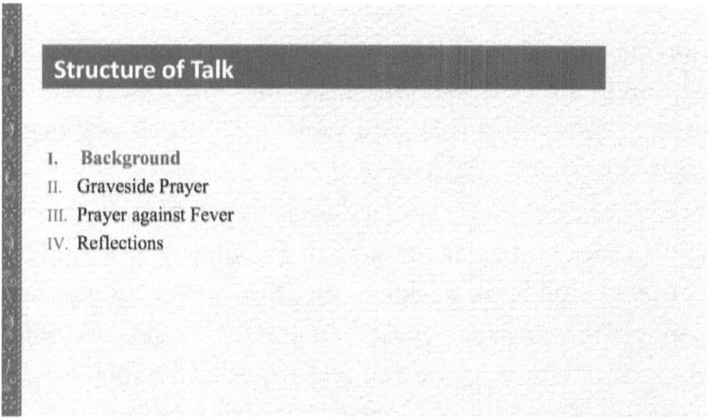

FIGURE 7. Slide from a talk by Elisheva Baumgarten, "Shared Appeals to Different Gods: Jews, Christians and Medieval Prayer," February 21, 2023. Image used with the permission of Elisheva Baumgarten.

words your audience will hear. Signposting is essential. Actual signs are not. Provide overviews and transitions verbally, using some of the formulas presented in chapter 3.

How to Design Slides

The best way to design slide content follows a method called Assertion-Evidence, developed by Joanna K. Garner and Michael P. Alley.[26]

26. Joanna K. Garner and Michael P. Alley, "How the Design of Presentation Slides Affects Audience Comprehension: A Case for the Assertion-Evidence Approach," *International Journal of Engineering Education* 29, no. 6 (2013): 1564–79. For a detailed account of an experiment that proves that Assertion-Evidence slides work better than slides formatted as bullet-point lists, see Wolfe et al., "Advancing the Knowledge Base on Effective Presentation Slide Design." For a broader discus-

Assertion: Create a headline that summarizes your assertion in eight words or less. It's a headline, so format your assertion in a very large font. **Make only one assertion per slide.** More than that and you will induce cognitive overload.

Evidence: Below the headline, show a picture, graph, table, chart, or diagram or have an accompanying sound recording or audiovisual clip ready. This is your *evidence*. Remember that any slide or clip you present should add something that words alone cannot. If you can explain your assertion effectively and compactly through words alone, then you don't need a slide. Any slide that contains only a headline is most likely a cue card prompting *you*, not material that your audience needs to understand what you're saying. People do not need to see a slide that states "Speech and text are processed in the same part of the brain" to understand you when you tell them that speech and text are processed in the same part of the brain. But they would benefit from seeing an image that highlights which part of the brain processes speech and text.

You've already seen an example of a slide designed according to these principles: Moshe Vardi's comparison of genetically modified pine versus natural pine, reproduced again in Figure 8. This slide provides a succinct five-word headline whose brevity leaves ample space for the image, which shows that natural pine is packed much more densely than genetically modified pine. Note that in this slide, the headline is not

---

sion of how to use the psychology of learning when designing slides, see Kosslyn, *Clear and to the Point*.

FIGURE 8. Slide from a talk by Moshe Y. Vardi, "Efficiency, Resilience, and Artificial Intelligence," March 24, 2025. Image used with the permission of Moshe Y. Vardi and the Institute for Advanced Study, School of Mathematics.

the assertion, which was that slower growth promotes greater resiliency. Vardi could have titled the slide "Growth vs. Resiliency," but instead, he left the assertion off the slide. Because nothing on the slide duplicated Vardi's explanation, listeners concentrated on what he had to say about how the image proved his point. Less is more.[27]

27. Moshe Y. Vardi, "Efficiency, Resilience, and Artificial Intelligence," Computer Science/Discrete Mathematics Seminar, Institute for Advanced Study, March 24, 2025, posted March 24, 2025, by @Institute for Advanced Study, YouTube video, 1:13:57, https://www.youtube.com/watch?v=Ji84f7eLxpU. If you want to see how a speaker delivers a talk where most of the slides follow the Assertion-Evidence template, I recommend Lin's talk "The Neural Substrates for Aggression." Dayu Lin, "The Neural Substrates for Aggression," Federation of European Neuroscience Societies Hertie Winter School 2018 on Neural Control of Instinctive and Innate Behaviour, Obergurgl, Austria, January 6–12, 2019, posted April 27, 2021,

If you're designing slides using the Assertion-Evidence template, **how should you present those slides when giving your talk?** Follow these precepts: **Show images, play non-verbal sounds, and speak words.** If you've put up a slide that does more than show your audience how to spell an unfamiliar word or name, talk people through *how* the slide or clip makes your point. The image might be a diagram, a chart, a graph, an equation, a reproduction of an object or work of art, a picture of an organism or compound, a page of musical notation, or a passage of text. Remember to read long passages aloud once *before* you show them and start to analyze them.

Never put detailed explanations on the slides themselves. Those explanations will be wordy and will compete with your spoken words, which will cause cognitive overload and encourage people to tune you out. A good rule of thumb is to use about ten spoken sentences to expand on each assertion that the image proves.[28]

If there's one thing I learned while writing this book, it's that people like to put lots of words on their slides, so it's worth highlighting the research that advises against this. In one experiment, researchers presented the same lecture, using an identical script, to 110 undergraduate engineering students. Fifty-nine saw a lecture that used Assertion-Evidence slides, and fifty-one saw a lecture that used slides with bullet lists. The fifty-nine students who viewed Assertion-Evidence slides wrote better essay

---

by @FENS, YouTube video, 42:44, https://www.youtube.com/watch?v=fZkHshEIp3s.

28. Garner and Alley, "How the Design of Presentation Slides Affects Audience Comprehension," 1568.

responses to open-ended questions, recalled key points from the lecture script more accurately, had a better understanding of the lecture topic, and developed more accurate mental models and a better understanding of the causal relationships involved in the topic. Students who viewed the lecture using Assertion-Evidence slides also found it easier to follow than the one that used slides with bullet lists. Why? Because Assertion-Evidence slides require presenters to identify and explain the key claim of each slide in ways that bullet lists do not.[29]

Okay, you'll say. Assertion-Evidence works for undergraduate students, but does it work for the experts who attend academic talks? Sometimes techniques that work well for less experienced learners backfire with more knowledgeable people.[30] To test for this "expertise reversal effect," one study asked an audience of faculty, PhD students, and industry experts to compare Assertion-Evidence slides with a range of other slide designs. The experts rated the presentations with Assertion-Evidence slides much higher than those with other kinds of slides, and none of their qualitative comments flagged the Assertion-Evidence format as quirky, unprofessional, or distracting.[31]

If Assertion-Evidence is the best way to design slides, why are slides with long bullet-point lists, detailed road maps, and large blocks of text so pervasive? For one thing, few academic

29. Wolfe et al., "Advancing the Knowledge Base on Effective Presentation Slide Design," 239.

30. Slava Kalyuga, Paul Ayres, Paul Chandler, and John Sweller, "The Expertise Reversal Effect," *Educational Psychologist* 38, no. 1 (2003): 23–31.

31. Wolfe et al., "Advancing the Knowledge Base on Effective Presentation Slide Design," 239.

speakers know the scientific literature on effective technical and professional communication.[32] Another reason ineffective slides are rife is that many academics design slides using PowerPoint, and for a long time, PowerPoint's default slide format was bullet-point lists.[33] Presenters didn't favor bullet lists because bullet lists aid comprehension and learning. They favored bullet lists because of inertia. Did the people who developed PowerPoint make bullet lists the default because they had proof of that format's effectiveness? They did not.[34]

Final Tips

I hope I have convinced you that slides work best when you use them to show what words alone cannot explain as effectively. Having offered a principle of slide design that has been proved to work well, I'll conclude with a few more tips about how to format and present essential slides.

32. Wolfe et al., "Advancing the Knowledge Base on Effective Presentation Slide Design," 236.

33. In 2013, 95 percent of the people creating computer presentations used PowerPoint to design roughly thirty million presentations per day; Garner and Alley, "How the Design of Presentation Slides Affects Audience Comprehension," 1565.

34. Gartner-Schmidt, "New Normal," 21S. Presentation software has changed since PowerPoint first came on the scene, but slides with bullet lists prevail across all the talks in my corpus. Nor are many of the recent changes to PowerPoint particularly effective. One study determines that PowerPoint's SmartArt slides consistently resulted in lower comprehension and recall than both text-only slides and Assertion-Evidence slides; Wolfe et al., "Advancing the Knowledge Base on Effective Presentation Slide Design," 248.

Label your slides. If you show an image of a microorganism or an asteroid or an ecosystem, include a label that lists both its scientific and popular names. If you show an image of an artwork, include a label that states who made it, where and when it was made, its actual size, and its current location. If you show an image of a historical document, include a label that states what it is and where you found it. If you put quotes on a slide (which, as noted above, you should do very sparingly), provide a full citation. Those citations should not identify the author by last name and date alone, because your audience has no idea what "Edelman 2016" means. Labels should include information such as photographer credits, but format that information in a smaller font unless it is essential to your argument.

Make sure your script indicates exactly when to put up a slide and when to take it down. You don't want to expend valuable mental energy keeping track of when to change slides while you are giving your talk. A script with clear instructions will also make it easier for you to ask someone else to manage your slides while you give your talk and will help you keep track of whether they are doing so correctly. Always practice showing your slides when you rehearse (see chapter 8).

Tell before you show. Give the audience a brief verbal preview *before* you show the slide. Do this even if you are using images on slides as memory prompts for yourself. People will better understand what you show them if you first tell them what to look for and how it matters. Cognitive scientists call this signaling: telling people how to process material before they see it.[35] For example, as noted earlier, before you play a music clip, tell your audience key elements to listen for. If you're transitioning from talking about the current economy to predictions about where it is heading, *first* say, "And that brings us to the future of inflation," *then* show a chart of what your economic model forecasts.

Begin by explaining what is on the slide. As soon as you put up a slide, explain it: "What you see here. . . ." If you are showing a chart, explain any color codes you are using. If you are showing a graph, define the axes. If you are showing equations, define the symbols. If you are showing images of a cell or star or plant or building or person, establish the basic facts: "This is the Taj Mahal, constructed between 1631 and 1648 as an emperor's memorial to his dead wife," then draw your audience's attention to how some less obvious and more surprising features related to your argument. "The reason I'm showing you this is. . . ." Never assume your audience will see what you see, even if it's right in front of them.

Face your audience while you discuss your slides. Some people like to move around the room while showing slides; some like to stand to the side of the screen. Do what feels good for you, but make sure to mostly face your audience so that they feel connected to you. Connection promotes attention.

Use a pointer. Make sure to have some way of singling out specific parts of the image. I prefer a physical pointer to a computer mouse because it's easier for the audience to see, easier for me to manage, and doesn't tether me to a device. Make

35. Mayer and Moreno, "Nine Ways to Reduce Cognitive Load in Multimedia Learning," 46.

sure to give your audience time to track where you point—you know where you're heading, but they don't, so they will lag a bit behind you.

If the details of a particular image are important, like the dragonfly in the unicorn tapestry mentioned earlier, create a separate slide that provides a magnified view of that detail so that audiences can see what you are analyzing.

In some cases, especially science talks, you may want to use a blackboard or whiteboard to show what a graph or equation would look like under alternative conditions.

Animations and builds can help direct audience attention. You can gradually highlight different components of a slide by adding color, arrows, text, or visual elements. But just because you can doesn't mean you should. If you don't already have expertise in graphic design and can't afford to hire a pro, adding these bells and whistles may take more time than they are worth. It is okay to use spoken words alone to emphasize which elements of a slide matter most and to explain what points they make.

Remove slides from view after you have finished discussing them. Keeping a slide up when you are no longer discussing it will distract your audience. After you are done explaining what is on the slide, if you don't have another slide to show immediately, shift to a blank slide, either black or white.

If you need to show a slide multiple times, copy it. Do not backtrack. It's distracting, even disorienting, to watch someone click back through a series of slides. Slide software makes it very easy to duplicate a slide within your presentation.

If you revise your talk after sending your presentation to the talk organizer, make sure that the slides remain in the

same order. If not, send the organizer a new version of your presentation. I witnessed at least one talk where the lecturer learned only when delivering their lecture that the version on the screen no longer corresponded to their script. I've also had this happen to me. If you know your material, you can usually salvage the situation, but it's even better to avoid it.

Back up your presentation in multiple formats. Back up your presentation on a keychain drive. Email it to yourself and to the organizer. Install your preferred presentation software on your phone and send your presentation to your phone (where you can usually also edit it). Upload your presentation to Dropbox or Google Drive and make sure to bring the sign-in info for those sites with you when you travel. Travel with printouts of all your slides so that even if some technical mishap means that your audience can't see them, you can still describe them.

Bring a universal dongle that connects your laptop to any kind of projection system. Connecting has gotten easier in recent years, but bringing your own dongle means it won't matter if you brought your presentation on a Mac laptop but your host institution only has a PC, or they can connect via USB but you need USC, or you are working in Keynote but the computer in the room where you're presenting only has PowerPoint.

Make sure that all text will be legible from anywhere in a large room. A good rule of thumb is to use a font size of sixteen points or higher. An audience member should be able to take a picture of your slide and be able to read it without magnification. The fewer words your slide contains, the easier this is to achieve.

Use larger text for assertions, definitions, and labels and smaller text for credits. Assertions are headlines. Stress their relative weight and importance by formatting them in large, heavy text. Definitions and labels—the meanings of your x- and y-axes or of the colors you use on a chart—provide vital information. Make sure everyone can read them. Less vital information should be assigned a smaller point size but still be legible to everyone in the room.

Use sans serif, medium-weight fonts such as Helvetica and Arial. These fonts are easiest to read on pixel-based screens (versus on the printed page).

Make your AV materials easy to comprehend. If you are sharing sound clips, make sure they are clearly audible. If you are sharing visual material, use the highest-resolution formats available. A low-resolution image that looks fine on your laptop may pixelate when you show it on a large screen. Use full-edge bleeds for graphics so that your slide has no margins.[36] If you must have a background, make it black for photos and white for text.

Finally, here's some further reading that offers detailed advice about effective data visualization and graphic design, which is a topic unto itself: Edward R. Tufte, *The Visual Display of Quantitative Information*; Stephen Kosslyn, *Clear and to the Point: 8 Psychological Principles for Compelling PowerPoint Presentations*; chapter 10, "Visuals: Those Slides Hurt!," in Chris Anderson, *TED Talks: The Official TED Guide to Public Speaking*, cowritten with Tom Rielly; Angela Riechers, *The Elements of Visual Grammar: A Designer's Guide for Writers,*

36. Gartner-Schmidt, "New Normal," 23S.

Scholars, and Professionals; and Jonathan Schwabish, *Better Data Visualizations: A Guide for Scholars, Researchers, and Wonks* and *Better Presentations: A Guide for Scholars, Researchers, and Wonks.*[37]

Slides are less necessary than most people think. While writing this book, I delivered a talk that had no slides to audiences in the United States, Australia, and Ireland. Each time, someone came up to me after I was done and said how refreshing it was to attend a talk that had no visuals. Scientists have shown that poorly designed slides actually obstruct learning.

Slides work well when used and designed properly. Use slides and clips to convey what words alone cannot: to share visual and audio material that constitutes your evidence; to spell out unfamiliar words your audience may not grasp just from sound alone; and to present large amounts of information that you have visualized compactly, including data, citations, and collaborators whom you want to credit. Never put a lot of text on a slide, unless that text is evidence you plan to speak about for at least twice as long as it takes you to read it aloud. In these cases, recite the text to your audience *before* you show it to them on a slide.

37. Edward R. Tufte, *The Visual Display of Quantitative Information*, 2nd ed. (Cheshire, CT: Graphics Press, 2001); Angela Riechers, *The Elements of Visual Grammar: A Designer's Guide for Writers, Scholars, and Professionals* (Princeton, NJ: Princeton University Press, 2024); Jonathan Schwabish, *Better Data Visualizations: A Guide for Scholars, Researchers, and Wonks* (New York: Columbia University Press, 2021).

If you do use slides, focus on showing images, not words. When your slides combine images and words, design them using the Assertion-Evidence principle: a brief headline of eight words or less, formatted in large, bold type, above an image that provides evidence of the assertion. Use words to explain exactly how the image is evidence for the assertion. Never place that explanation on the slide itself; talk your audience through it.

Make sure your audience can easily see and hear any and all AV materials that you present. Formatting slides requires understanding technical principles of graphic design, so consult specialized guides when preparing complex charts and graphs.

Finally, if you want to watch some examples of academic talks that use slides to excellent effect, I recommend "The Neural Substrates for Aggression" by Dayu Lin, "Bitten: Why Are Some People More Attractive to Mosquitoes than Others?" by Leslie B. Vosshall, "Dürer's Mobility" by Joseph Koerner, and "Shared Appeals to Different Gods: Jews, Christians and Medieval Prayer" by Elisheva Baumgarten.[38]

38. Lin, "Neural Substrates for Aggression"; Leslie B. Vosshall, "Bitten: Why Are Some People More Attractive to Mosquitoes than Others?," NIH Director's Wednesday Afternoon Lecture Series, National Institutes of Health, October 26, 2022, posted October 28, 2022, by @NIH VideoCast, YouTube video, 1:00:10, https://www.youtube.com/watch?v=XNUlwMfqClg; Koerner, "Dürer's Mobility"; Baumgarten, "Shared Appeals to Different Gods."

7

Delivery

YOU DELIVER a talk using your body, especially your voice. In extraordinary circumstances someone else may deliver your talk for you—but they will do so using their body, especially their voice.

To deliver talks well, it helps to be able to control your voice. To control your voice, you need to work with your breath. To work with your breath, you need to have good posture, which has the added benefit of making a good impression. A sense of when and how to gesture and move around the room will also affect what is, at the end of the day, a performance.

This chapter explains what works best in terms of posture, breathing, gestures, and facial expressions, as well as vocal intensity, pitch, speed, rhythm, articulation, and tone. But to actually learn *how* to do what works, you will need to devote a few hours to practicing these things *in person,* under the guidance of a trained professional. That trained professional can be a voice coach, a theater director, a speech therapist, or some combination of those. Reading about effective delivery will not suffice, nor will working with apps or watching videos, although apps and videos can help reinforce what a trained professional has taught you.

Finding a coach requires a bit of research, but it's worth it: in three reasonably priced hours, you will improve your presentation skills in ways you can't achieve on your own. Vocal training is a physical skill—a praxis. As Aristotle wrote long ago, we acquire practical knowledge through action. We learn how to swim by swimming, how to play basketball by playing basketball. However, when swimming, we know if we are sinking or afloat. It's similarly obvious whether a ball makes a basket or doesn't. It's much more difficult to perceive our voices accurately, even harder to figure out how to adjust them. That's where a professional can help.

Each of us has a distinctive facial structure and vocal apparatus that influences how loudly and resonantly we can speak. A trained voice coach or speech therapist understands how to leverage an individual's unique strengths and work around any built-in limitations. A voice teacher, for example, can identify that a particular person will be more audible if they slightly raise their pitch and that they can achieve that by subtly lowering their chin. Another person, with a different vocal apparatus, may need to raise their chin to achieve the same effect or should be aiming to lower their pitch, not raise it.

In an ideal world, academic departments would offer voice training workshops for graduate students, but few do. Most universities and colleges do, however, have theater programs and music departments, and you can start your search for a voice coach there, as well as for a director who can help you think about how to stand and gesture when delivering your talk. Most schools also offer access to gyms and exercise classes; use them if you can. Swimming, yoga, running, and team sports are all great ways to work on breathing, posture, and the kind of body awareness that will help you make the micro-adjustments needed to improve delivery. If those aren't for you, walking also helps. The ancient Greek orator Demosthenes, endowed with no innate talent as a speaker, reportedly practiced declaiming his speeches while running along the beach and yelling above the roar of the ocean. As a result, he had more than enough lung capacity, stamina, and volume to deliver his speeches under regular conditions.[1]

Demosthenes also practiced speaking with pebbles in his mouth so that articulating without them would feel easier. I don't recommend that, but I do recommend that at some point you challenge yourself to do some kind of performance that scares you even more than giving an academic lecture. Read your own poetry at an open mic, do stand-up comedy or improv, sing karaoke while stone-cold sober, perform in a community theater production—anything that requires you to use your body and voice and triggers even more anxiety than giving an academic lecture.

For a few years, I took singing lessons and performed at student recitals. Doing so helped me practice modulating my breathing, loudness, pitch, and pace in a situation I found way scarier than delivering an academic talk. Those performances

1. Whatever their basis in actual fact, Demosthenes anecdotes feature frequently in articles on effective speaking. See, e.g., Patrick C. Friman, "Behavior Analysts to the Front! A 15- Step Tutorial on Public Speaking," *Behavioral Analyst* 37 (2014), 112.

helped me become a better speaker not because they went well but because they went pretty badly. Five years of voice lessons took my singing from awful to mediocre. But my speaking benefited immensely. I found it much easier to implement techniques for achieving better vocal resonance and breath control when I was just talking and not also trying to manage key changes, tamp down my vibrato, and remember the third verse of "Diamonds Are a Girl's Best Friend." The psychological benefits were even bigger. Performing "Have You Met Miss Jones?" completely off-key while a roomful of strangers stared at me with polite pity was mortifying, but it also helped me recognize my relative competence as an academic speaker. Now, before I begin a lecture, I soothe my nerves by taking five deep breaths while telling myself, "At least I don't have to sing this!"

Again, reading this chapter can't teach you *how* to acquire better speech technique. Instead, it breaks down *what* you can improve. Below is a checklist of skills that you can share with potential coaches to determine whether they can help you achieve your specific goals. You can also use this checklist when annotating your talk for delivery (see chapter 8, "Rehearsal") and give it to a test audience to structure their feedback on your practice talk. As with all my advice throughout this book, follow these recommendations to the extent that you can, and adapt them to your specific needs and circumstances, including any disabilities or access requirements.

Posture. Good posture will make you look *and* feel more confident, purposeful, and open. It will also help you breathe more effectively, which is important for staying calm and being audible. Good posture is not easy to achieve, especially for anyone whose job requires a lot of time at a computer. Whether you deliver your talk standing or sitting, pull your shoulders a little more back and down, lift your torso, and work on centering your head and evenly distributing your weight.

Breathing. Every expert advises speakers to be as present as possible. Why? Because the more present *you* are, the more engaged and present your audience will be.[2]

Presence is as an elusive concept, so I suggest focusing on something more palpable: breathing. Learn to breathe consistently; many of us hold our breath without even realizing it. Learn to breathe deeply. Very deeply—lung tissue extends into the back, so when you fill your lungs, really fill them. A trained coach will be able to help you pinpoint whether you're fully tanking up and which techniques will help you do so.

Breathing deeply will help you sound more present by anchoring and supporting your voice. Speech is powered by breath, so the deeper you breathe, the louder, longer, and more clearly you can speak.[3] Breathing deeply also helps you *feel* more present because deep breaths calm the nervous system, especially when we exhale for longer than we inhale. Inhaling makes your heart speed up, exhaling slows it down, so longer exhales calm the heart flutters many of us experience when speaking in public. Making your exhales longer than your inhales also activates your parasympathetic nervous

2. Friman, "Behavior Analysts to the Front!," 115.

3. "The Interrelationship of Breathing and Speaking," *Today* (blog), June 30, 2022, Icahn School of Medicine at Mount Sinai, https://health.mountsinai.org/blog/the-interelationship-of-breathing-and-speaking/.

system, easing you out of high-stress fight-or-flight mode into a mellower rest-and-digest groove.

If you want to practice this, start by inhaling for a count of four and exhaling for eight, then extend that. When I give talks, I do 4:8 breathing while my host introduces me. I find that more soothing than listening to myself being talked about in the third person or worrying about how my audience is going to respond to my ideas. You're not a worrier? Great. Do the 4:8 breathing to get your lungs in gear before you start.

Once your talk gets started, you can't do 4:8 breathing, but it's helpful to keep taking full breaths, especially when you pause between sentences. Singing lessons are a great way to learn how to inhale deeply very quickly, then exhale evenly and lightly, budgeting your breath so that you can speak even long sentences without running out of oxygen. Of course, as noted in chapters 2 and 8, your sentences should never be so long that you can't deliver them in one steady breath. If you're having trouble saying something without running out of breath, rewrite it.

Bodily gestures and facial expressions. Learn to hold your body in ways that put you at ease and express confidence. Doing so has the added benefits of relaxing your audience and holding their attention. To see this in action, I recommend watching Daniel Larson's talk "Understanding Transcription and Splicing Heterogeneity in Cancer Progression," delivered at the Koch Institute in 2017.[4] From the moment Larson

4. Daniel R. Larson, "Understanding Transcription and Splicing Heterogeneity in Cancer Progression," Koch Institute Symposium 2017, Koch Institute for Integrative Cancer Research, MIT, June 16, 2017, posted July 8, 2017, by

began, even when fiddling with his tech, he appeared focused, deliberate, and connected to himself and his audience—*present*. His body and voice radiated energy and enthusiasm about his ideas and about the act of sharing them. Even when I didn't understand some of his more technical points, I felt energized and engaged listening to him make them.

A good director will help you figure out what works best for you, but here are some easy and underused techniques for using your body when delivering a talk.[5]

Use motion and stillness to underscore your points. Hand movements and walking around the front of the room are effective ways to retain audience attention and underscore important points. If you like delivering talks on the move, you can underscore important points by speeding up, slowing down, or subtly increasing or decreasing your step length. A good way to prepare the audience for a crucial point is to come to a complete halt just before making it.[6]

Another use of motion to dramatic effect is to draw a bit closer to your audience or take a step back from it.

Subtle uses of motion: vary your eye contact by meeting the gaze of more or fewer audience members or by holding that eye contact for a bit longer or shorter than your baseline. Or take a sip of water when transitioning from one section of your talk to another.

@KochInstituteMIT, YouTube video, 26:28, https://www.youtube.com/watch?v=7yHmB_yXBFE.

5. On underuse of basic good speaking techniques, see Valentina Ryndak, et. al., "Actualization of the Problem of Forming the Public Speaking Experience," *Revista de Investigaciones Universidad del Quindio* 34 (2022) 105-6.

6. See Anderson, *TED Talks*, 207.

Use facial expressions and gestures as punctuation. A raised eyebrow, slightly widened eyes, or hint of a smile can all serve as nonverbal punctuation. Sophie Smith's lecture "The Nature of Politics," delivered at Cambridge University in 2017, is a great example of how even very subtle facial expressions can dramatize logical turns in a presentation. Academic talks should never be too dramatic, and Smith's talk is instructive because she was the antithesis of a showboater. She opened with an anecdote about her mother telling her she needed to speak with more "oomph," and during her prefatory remarks, delivered extemporaneously, she did come off as quite muted. Yet she found ways to work with that low-key baseline, such as opening her eyes a bit wider when she transitioned from the "They say" to the "I say" portion of her talk, to excellent effect.[7]

Facial expressions and gestures can do more than intensify words; they can also substitute for them. A bit of mime can help audiences visualize crucial information, as when Leslie Vosshall, in a riveting talk on mosquitoes, used her arms to show how mosquitoes brace themselves on human skin.[8] She could have just shown us a video of a mosquito (and later

7. Sophie Smith, "The Nature of Politics," Quentin Skinner Lecture and Symposium, Centre for Research in the Arts, Social Sciences and Humanities, Cambridge University, June 9, 2017, posted June 15, 2017, by @CRASSH Cambridge, YouTube video, 1:04:09, https://www.youtube.com/watch?v=si9iG-093aY.

8. Leslie B. Vosshall, "Bitten: Why Are Some People More Attractive to Mosquitoes than Others?," NIH Director's Wednesday Afternoon Lecture Series, National Institutes of Health, October 26, 2022, posted October 28, 2022, by @NIH VideoCast, YouTube video, 1:00:10, https://www.youtube.com/watch?v=XNUlwMfqClg.

did—it was scary), but it was easier for us to see the motion, and viscerally *feel* it, when the human at the front of the room modeled it.

Consider ways *not* to use your face and body. It's also important to think about what you could *stop* doing with your face, voice, and body. Are you smirking even when you aim to be sincere? Talking for long stretches with your eyes completely closed? Ending most of your sentences by drily laughing "ha ha ha"? We often do these things without realizing we're doing them. When other people notice us doing them, they rarely say anything, for fear of upsetting us. At your dress rehearsals, tell the friends in your test audience to flag any tics, and reassure them that you'll be grateful, not offended, when they point them out.

Some movements are good, but certain movements risk distracting some people in your audience. Do not sway, do not rock, do not shift constantly from one foot to the other. Do not fiddle with rings, necklaces, bracelets, and name tags; do not jangle pocket change or keys; do not drum your fingers on the podium or desk; do not click your pen; do not play with your hair. Doing these things may soothe you, and some audience members will be oblivious to these gestures, but your job is to focus on the audience, and some people will find these movements and sounds very distracting.

Eliminate verbal tics and filler. This may take time to achieve, so don't get so hung up on it that you feel inhibited. But it is important. Record yourself and listen to the recordings. Ask people in your test audience to attend to your speech patterns, especially when answering questions, when you may be the most nervous and the least scripted. A very common verbal tic is using "um" and "uh" as filler. Some scientists have found that audiences respond well to the judicious use of filler words because they create pauses, which in turn improve audience engagement and comprehension.[9] Um, sure. Here's a better way to do that: train yourself to actually pause instead of using filler sounds to do so.[10]

Filler words such as "like," "you know," and "well" don't tend to make a good impression.[11] Without making a bugbear of it, try to weed these phrases from your unscripted speech. Another verbal tic to avoid: ending sentences with "right?" or "okay?" The rule of thumb: if you wouldn't add these words to the published version of your talk, avoid them when you speak. Words like "so," "basically," and "actually" do appear in writing and can make your talk sound more conversational. Use them—but don't overuse them, because turned into repetitive tics that end almost every sentence, these otherwise useful transition words may cause some audience members to tune you out.

Manage your audibility. It's not a talk if people can't hear you. We usually refer to volume or loudness when discussing audibility. What actually matters is your voice's *intensity*: how loud your sound remains as it moves through space, measured

9. Valerie Fridland and Ruth Gotian, "Linguistic Tricks to Grab an Online Audience's Attention," *Nature* 591 (2021): S42.

10. For some exercises to help speakers increase the use of pauses, see chapter 4 of Bill Hoogterp, *Your Perfect Presentation: Speak in Front of Any Audience Anywhere and Never Be Nervous Again* (New York: McGraw Hill, 2014).

11. Research suggests this may be especially true for older audience members. On generational differences in perceptions of speech patterns, see Fridland and Gotian, "Linguistic Tricks to Grab an Online Audience's Attention," S42.

as decibels over square feet. In other words, what's loud in your small office may not be loud to the people at the back of a large lecture hall. To achieve the right intensity for larger venues requires that you increase the *energy* of your sound waves, which is their amplitude over time—and there's a nice, nerdy technical issue to work on with your voice coach. Microphones can help with this, but you can't count on always having access to one that works or on being able to use a particular microphone effectively.

Many of us, for personal and cultural reasons, find it difficult to speak with intensity. If you worry that speaking with intensity comes off as overbearing or arrogant, reframe that: speaking audibly expresses care and consideration for your audience by making it easy for them to hear you and to understand what you are saying. As Robert Mawhinney noted in our interview, audiences in the United States conventionally expect speakers to talk loudly and somewhat expressively. "When you're the speaker, that's your role." My experience is limited, but I've found the same preferences in France, India, China, Brazil, Ireland, Germany, Austria, and Belgium, though it's also the case that scholars the world over accept a wide range of presentation styles. It's absolutely fine to be low-key and restrained, so long as you are audible. Remember that you're not projecting your voice for personal reasons. You're projecting your voice because it's your job.

Increasing your vocal intensity is the single most important thing you can do to deliver your talk effectively. This is the conclusion of a 2015 study that measured the effects of intensity, pitch, speech rate, articulation rate, speaker head movement, and speaker motion. And I mean *measured*, using tools such as an AutoBi Intensity Extractor. Even better, this study tested speaker effectiveness using two different metrics: they asked audiences to rate speakers *and* they separately measured actual levels of audience engagement—an imperfect science, but a useful supplement to audience self-reporting. Best of all: while much of the research on effective speaking focuses on undergraduate classrooms, this study focused on speakers at an academic conference, with most delivering their talks individually while standing behind a podium and addressing an audience seated in front of them.[12]

Their finding: the speaker's vocal intensity was the only metric that correlated both with higher audience ratings *and* with increased actual engagement. "Increasing levels of intensity correspond to increasing levels of involvement."[13] This is great to know because it tells us what to prioritize when working on our delivery. Lecturers also want to make a good impression, and increased intensity helps with that, too; audiences attribute confidence and conviction to people who speak loudly.[14] Vocal intensity doesn't mean being emo and extreme; it's just a technical term for loudness that lasts. Simply put, **your audience feels at ease, and attributes ease to**

12. Keith Curtis, Gareth J. F. Jones, and Nick Campbell, "Effects of Good Speaking Techniques on Audience Engagement," in *Proceedings of the 2015 ACM on International Conference on Multimodal Interaction* (New York: Association for Computing Machinery, 2015), 35–42, https://doi.org/10.1145/2818346.2820766.

13. Curtis et al., "Effects of Good Speaking Techniques on Audience Engagement," 41.

14. Alex B. Van Zant and Jonah Berger, "How the Voice Persuades," *Journal of Personality and Social Psychology: Interpersonal Relations and Group Processes* 118, no. 4 (2020): 663.

you, when they can easily hear you. Unless your test audiences tell you that you are speaking way too loudly (a rarity, but it happens), assume that you can always turn the vocal intensity up a bit.

A microphone is a great way to increase speech intensity. However, you can't always count on one being available or working when it is. Sometimes the room will only have a fixed mic, but you will want to move around. A mic can also be ineffective when it's the kind that amplifies you only if you position your mouth directly in front of it, which can be difficult to sustain for fifty minutes. When I've used these, I've often heard myself go from VERY LOUD to *very soft* whenever I turned my head even a tiny bit. In those situations, it's good to be able to make yourself heard even without a mic, which most people can achieve with coaching and practice.

Managing your voice's intensity is not just a matter of sustaining the same exact level of loudness throughout your entire talk. Change captures people's attention, so occasionally *varying* how loudly you speak also helps keep your audience alert.[15] Saying words loudly emphasizes them, so deliver key phrases with a bit more intensity. Slightly decreasing your vocal intensity can inject emotion or create suspense. Small increases or decreases in vocal intensity can underscore a point or demarcate the items in a numbered list. For a good example of this, I recommend watching Michal Bassani-Sternberg's talk on cancer vaccines.[16] A good director will

15. Van Zant and Berger, "How the Voice Persuades," 676.

16. Michal Bassani-Sternberg, "Antigen Discovery for Development of Personalized Cancer Vaccines," Koch Institute Symposium 2023, Koch Institute for

help you identify when it works best to make these small adjustments. As the next chapter explains, you can annotate your text for dynamics, just as singers mark crescendos and diminuendos on their scores.

Manage your pitch. Scientists have proved that the acoustic properties of speech—what they call paralanguage—affect how people react to spoken talks. A lot. There's a reason that "monotonous" is a synonym for "boring." Varying the notes on which you speak can keep audiences alert. This doesn't mean you have to be a big ham; when delivering an academic talk, very small pitch changes go a long way. In fact, coming on too strong makes most audiences wary, especially if they feel you are trying too hard to persuade them.[17] But this does mean that you can communicate a lot by subtly varying your pitch and rhythm, matching your tone to your topic. Rex Harrison in the musical *My Fair Lady* is a famous example of vocalization that hovers between singing and speech. According to Wikipedia, other examples include Lou Reed, Billie Eilish, and Olivia Rodrigo.[18]

Some pitch changes are to be avoided, especially uptalk and vocal fry. Uptalk means ending a sentence by raising one's pitch. English speakers typically raise their pitch when posing questions, so experts counsel against using uptalk for declarative sentences because it makes speakers sound unsure of their own statements. Vocal fry involves speaking in a very low

---

Integrative Cancer Research, MIT, June 23, 2023, posted July 12, 2023, by @KochInstituteMIT, YouTube video, 1:04:25, https://www.youtube.com/watch?v=0GMl1G4M-0o.

17. Van Zant and Berger, "How the Voice Persuades," 662.

18. "*Sprechgesang*," Wikipedia, https://en.wikipedia.org/wiki/Sprechgesang.

register and closing one's vocal cords completely, then popping them back open, which results in a rough and crinkly sound. Experts counsel against this because over the course of a long talk it can fatigue the vocal cords and because it's often less audible than speech in a higher register. Some people like uptalk and vocal fry; some people don't, so you decide whether you want to try to change these things if you are doing them.

Manage your speed. Most experts recommend delivering a talk at about 130 words per minute. It's common to speed up when nervous, so unless your test audiences have told you that you are speaking too slowly, aim to speak more slowly than you *think* you need to speak. If you want a more objective way to test this, record yourself. You should sound normal even if you speed up the recording to play at 1.25 speed.

I've heard many talks where lecturers spoke so quickly that I often missed key words or entire points, especially when I was taking notes. Conversely, though by temperament I value speed and efficiency, I found myself consistently impressed by those who spoke in ways I perceived as quite slow. Good examples of this in my corpus are the talks "Do Whales Judge Us?" by Bathsheba Demuth, "Intimate Inequalities" by Brodwyn Fischer, and "Countering Culture" by Jaimie Baron.[19]

19. Bathsheba Demuth, "Do Whales Judge Us? Interspecies History and Ethics," Environment Forum, Mahindra Humanities Center, Harvard University, November 6, 2019, posted December 5, 2019, by @Harvard University, YouTube video, 1:51:47, https://www.youtube.com/watch?v=yh_kJA0Naug; Brodwyn Fischer, "Intimate Inequalities," Radcliffe Institute for Advanced Study at Harvard University, September 26, 2022, posted March 31, 2023, by @Harvard Radcliffe Institute, YouTube video, 59:51, https://www.youtube.com/watch?v=0TGMm6LASrU; Jaimie Baron, "Countering Culture: Shirley Clarke and the Edges of Cinema,"

Their slowness was dramatic, but none of these speakers came across as overly theatrical. Instead, their deliberate, unhurried pace made them seem thoughtful and helped me focus on what they were saying for the duration of their talks.

It's good to sound excited about your material, and it is possible to combine slowness and passion. Robert Waldinger did that in his book talk "The Good Life." Waldinger's calm voice and intent focus kept me riveted the entire time he spoke, even though I was already familiar with the ideas he was presenting. As befits a practicing psychoanalyst who is also a Zen priest, Waldinger never rushed or sped up, even when told that he was running out of time. Throughout, he stayed present in his body, voice, and material. One of Waldinger's key points was that "the clearest expression of love is the gift of undivided attention," and he applied that insight to his delivery. His unwavering attention to the act of communicating his research findings secured mine; his measured, unhurried pace was a key way that he performed attentiveness.[20]

It's especially crucial to speak slowly if your audience is multilingual or if you are delivering your talk in a language that isn't your first. Another situation that calls for a slower pace: delivering material in multiple languages, as might

---

Radcliffe Institute for Advanced Study at Harvard University, March 29, 2023, posted April 6, 2023, by @Harvard Radcliffe Institute, YouTube video, 59:19, https://www.youtube.com/watch?v=YUqEnb6HkUE.

20. Robert Waldinger, "The Good Life," Lee Kum Sheung Center for Health and Happiness, T. H. Chan School for Public Health, Harvard University, February 27, 2023, posted February 28, 2023, by @Lee Kum Sheung Center for Health and Happiness, YouTube video, 1:02:27, https://www.youtube.com/watch?v=HUHowWFJNBg.

happen, for example, if you are lecturing about Spanish literature in English. Switching between two languages requires extra cognitive effort even for audiences fluent in both.

To dramatize a point, **vary your speed**. Don't overdo this—in most academic settings, it's not effective to sound too oratorical or dramatic. But if something is very important, don't just say it twice (as counseled in chapter 3). Say it very slowly. Conversely, to convey the urgency of a point you are about to make, try speeding up slightly. Most dramatic of all, of course, are pauses and full stops, which will instantly activate your audience's attention and also allow you and your audience to take a breath. For a great example of this, I once again recommend watching Sophie Smith's lecture "The Nature of Politics" to observe how judiciously she used pauses to dramatize key turns in her argument.

How do you know when to pause? If you're reading a prepared text, you've already figured this out. Short stops correspond to commas, semicolons, and colons; hard stops correspond to periods and paragraph breaks; longer pauses correspond to section breaks or sentences you've bolded or italicized. As David Levine said in our interview, your delivery should "respect the distinction between each kind of stop." Pause longer for a period than for a comma, longer for a section break than for a period. Or as Branden Joseph put it, "Read the punctuation." Whether you are annotating a fully scripted talk or working from slides and notes, if you don't intuitively know when to speed up, slow down, or come to a brief full stop, insert cues to remind you when to do so—as most of the expert speakers I interviewed reported doing when delivering their own talks and as detailed in the next chapter on rehearsal.

Improve your articulation. Technically, articulation refers to the number of syllables per phonation time—how much time you spend on each sound you utter. Articulation subjectively impacts how audiences perceive you and objectively affects how well they can hear you. A faster articulation rate is often perceived as fluency, since it involves being able to coordinate breathing and vocalizing with using one's tongue, teeth, and lips.[21] When you practice tongue twisters like "If Peter Piper picked a peck of peppers, how many peppers did Peter Piper pick," articulation is one of the skills you're honing.

Colloquially, articulation refers to how crisply you speak—how well people can distinguish one syllable from another when you talk. I don't recommend getting too preoccupied with this, but most of us have one or two consonants we could clean up; for me, it's double *t*'s. A good vocal coach will offer easy fixes for your particular issues. In my case, I had to learn to position my tongue a bit higher when pronouncing words like "mitten" and "kitten"—or, more relevantly for my research expertise, "written."

Articulation also includes pronunciation. Look up the correct way to say key names, terms, and words in your talk. Names can be especially difficult for people to understand, even when pronounced correctly, because it's often hard to fill them in from context. As noted in chapter 6, err on the side of placing important names on slides or handouts and slowing

21. Victoria Tumanova, Patricia M. Zebrowski, Rebecca N. Throneburg, and Mavis E. Kulak Kayikci, "Articulation Rate and Its Relationship to Disfluency Type, Duration, and Temperament in Preschool Children Who Stutter," *Journal of Communication Disorders* 44, no. 1 (2011): 116–29, https://doi.org/10.1016/j.jcomdis.2010.09.001.

down to pronounce them. Don't take for granted that you know how to pronounce a word just because you know how to spell it. I know an academic who could spot a typo from miles away but had been mispronouncing the word "pedant" for years. Ever since I pointed out that error to them, they've made sure to alert me to every word I mispronounce—which happens more often than I'd have predicted. Thankfully, none of those words were harmed while either of us were giving talks, and I now err on the side of checking pronunciation.

Learn to feel the rhythm of your sentences. Prose as well as poetry has rhythm, and good prose writers craft sentences with distinctive cadences. If you want to learn more about this, I recommend Herbert Read's *English Prose Style,* first published in 1928.[22] Though Read's work applies most directly to talks delivered in English, it can help attune you to any language. I love *English Prose Style* so much that I wrote an Amazon review that compared reading it with "getting to be alone, at night, in a museum where the artworks are great sentences and paragraphs." I love this book so much that once, when I was invited to a party where each guest had been asked to bring their favorite book, I brought *English Prose Style,* to the befuddlement of fellow partygoers toting copies of *Siddhartha* and *The Hitchhiker's Guide to the Galaxy*. I stand by my choice: it's full of sentences that sing. Like a musical line, a sentence has a beat and a pulse, a tension and an energy, and a good speaker finds and sustains those rhythms.

22. Herbert Read, *English Prose Style* (London: G. Bell and Sons, 1928), https://archive.org/details/in.ernet.dli.2015.113659.

Attend to your tone. Tone refers to how your inflections interpret your words. Do you sound sarcastic, earnest, surprised, inviting, puzzled? While you don't want to overdo any kind of tone in an academic setting, it's helpful when tone matches and reinforces content. For example, if you are talking about the harmful effects of homelessness, or images of human sacrifice, it's a bit odd to do so in a flat, dull voice. No matter what your topic, if you sound bored and disengaged, your audience will feel the same way.

Tone also conveys emphasis and offers cues about your talk's logical structure. If you're speaking from a text, deliver anything in italics or bold with a slight shift in tone. Changes in tone can also reinforce or even substitute for signposting, as I learned in listening to Franziska Michor's talk on computational models of cancer.[23] Michor almost never explicitly flagged which of her points mattered most or announced that she was transitioning from one topic to another, but her tone consistently alerted me to what she considered her most important methods, questions, and findings.

If your talk involves quoting an interview respondent, in addition to stating, "I'm going to use X's words here," you might also modulate your tone to signal the shift from your voice to theirs.

Finally, tone communicates your emotional connection to your material and how you feel about presenting it. Don't feel

23. Franziska Michor, "Computational Models of Cancer," Koch Institute Symposium 2017, Koch Institute for Integrative Cancer Research, MIT, June 16, 2017, posted July 8, 2017, by @KochInstituteMIT, YouTube video, 20:36, https://www.youtube.com/watch?v=rqtYLg8OZ8I.

that you have to overperform confidence. Many of the best speakers in my corpus took an understated approach. Most academic audience members know, as Robert Mawhinney put it, "not to mistake confidence or arrogance for ability. . . . This is not a bravado contest." Some people even sound too confident and need to learn to tone that down.

In ways that suit your individual personality and your specific material, aim for a tone that conveys enthusiasm: how interested you are in what you are saying and in the act of saying it. If you connect to your ideas and to your body, voice, and words, your audience will connect to your talk.

Delivering a good talk involves your body as well as your mind. To improve your physical delivery skills, it helps to work with a coach who can observe you and offer technical pointers. I've had graduate students report and show significant progress after only three sessions. Even a few small adjustments can make a big difference in how audible and engaging you sound and how confident and calm you feel.

What critic Roland Barthes called "the grain of the voice" is gloriously individual.[24] The aim of this chapter has been to help you inhabit your specific, unique voice more intentionally and fully, so that you can sound the way you want to sound.

24. Roland Barthes, "The Grain of the Voice," in *Image—Music—Text*, trans. Stephen Heath (New York: Hill & Wang, 1977), 179–89.

Keep in mind, however, that the physiology of breathing doesn't vary much from person to person. To deliver a talk effectively, it helps to fill your lungs completely, exhale for longer than you inhale, and do your best to align your head, neck, and torso. All of this will help you project your voice with more intensity, which will make it easier for audiences to hear what you are saying and connect to the ideas you are presenting.

If you want to develop your confidence when delivering academic talks, consider dabbling in other ways of performing that you find more daunting. I know it sounds a bit zany, and your amateur attempts at a tight five comic set or belting out "My Way" will probably flop. But they will boost your confidence as an academic speaker. If you're already very self-assured, experimenting with other forms of public performance may teach you something you can use in your scholarly presentations. If you're prone to stage fright, performing in an unfamiliar setting can provide visceral proof that everything is relative and you are better at delivering academic thoughts than you realized.

The recommendations in this chapter are foundational, but you can experiment with them at any point in your career. It's never too late to build more gestures into a talk, experiment with variations in pitch and pace, or practice speaking with more intensity. No matter what your career stage, however, there is one thing that every academic speaker must do: rehearse a talk thoroughly before delivering it for the first time. How best to do that is the subject of the next chapter.

8

Rehearsal

WHY REHEARSE?

Let's start with a very corny joke. A tourist visiting New York City stops someone on a busy street and asks, "How do you get to Carnegie Hall?" The answer: "Practice, practice, practice."

To give an effective talk, you must practice delivering it many times before you take it on the road. Not rehearsing is not an option. Let's get that myth out of the way immediately. Many of us have heard colleagues at conferences brag about writing their talks on the plane just hours before delivering them or just scribbling some notes on the back of an envelope. Do not listen to them. They either are exaggerating, are lying, or give terrible talks.[1]

1. As Patrick C. Friman notes, fearless speakers who do not rehearse are usually overconfident, and overconfidence makes them impervious to their own poor performances: "This condition is not so much a problem for them as it is for their audiences," who must endure the mediocre results ("Behavior Analysts to the Front!," 111). To be sure, we all know a few people who do a great job with very little

If anyone could get away with giving a talk impromptu, it's the seasoned scholars I interviewed while writing this book. Instead, each of them said the same thing: if you want to give a good academic talk, you must rehearse. Michèle Lamont told me: "Rehearsing is absolutely crucial. . . . You cannot go in cold." Branden Joseph noted: "I always tell students, rehearse your talk." Mariana Alessandri stated: "You have to practice." David Levine simply said: "Rehearse."

A talk is a performance. As the previous chapter on delivery explained, performing one's talk involves more than simply reading or reciting one's lines. In our interview, Nicholas Dames broke this down: There is the script, there is our embodiment of that script, there may be slides and other peripherals to maneuver, and there is an audience to handle. Robert Mawhinney concurred: "Talks require people to juggle a lot, and practice is the best way to get more proficient." Mariana Alessandri made the same point: "Giving a talk is . . . like a performance, and I think we often don't take it seriously as a performance. You have to work on your voice. You have to say it like you mean it; inflect; make eye contact." Only by running through your talk several times before delivering it will you be able to integrate these many different elements into a cohesive performance.

To give a talk is to be the center of attention, and many of us feel uncomfortable with that—so much so that, as I discussed in chapter 3, we often show up to our talks armored and nervous, which makes our audience armored and nervous as

---

preparation. You're probably not one of them, and even if you are, practicing will make you even better.

well. Practicing your talk makes you more familiar with your material *and* helps you feel more at ease with yourself. Both will help you relate well to your audience. "Practice produces fluency and fluency underlies mastery."[2] Mastery is not domination. Mastery means feeling present, connected to your ideas and to the words that convey them, to the body you use to express them, and to the people who have gathered to hear you. It's hard to feel present and connected to your ideas, words, body, and audience if you are stumbling over your sentences or worrying about exceeding your allotted time.

David Levine recommended reading a paper aloud at least twice before delivering it. There's no harm in exceeding that. Every time you read your talk aloud, you internalize it better, which makes it easier to look away from your notes, text, and slides to make eye contact with your audience and get a sense of how they are responding. The more you have rehearsed, Levine observed, "the more you can check in with how people are doing." As Daniel Immerwahr put it, "It's quite dangerous if you are not present with the people in the room and attuned to their responses. . . . It's very hard to hit a target if you are not looking at the target." How can you free yourself up to look at your target while delivering your talk? Practice, practice, practice.

Why do people so often not rehearse, even when they know it's a good idea and have plenty of time to do so? It's hard to say, but I would speculate that there are two main reasons: boredom and fear. It can be tedious to run through an entire talk with no audience present. If you find rehearsing tedious,

2. Friman, "Behavior Analysts to the Front!," 111.

it is. Consider using a reward system to motivate yourself. (I hear that people like chocolate.) Another trick for making rehearsals less tedious is to record them. This creates an audience for your rehearsal—yourself, watching the playback after rehearsal ends, which will also help you identify areas to improve.

Fear can be a more complicated block. The research on public speaking is full of references to surveys showing that people fear public speaking more than they fear snakes.[3] (The bright side: even herpetologists are unlikely ever to have to address a room filled with writhing, hissing serpents.) Many academics report feeling their heart flutter while delivering lectures. Some people even feel nauseated when giving presentations, and we've all seen speakers deliver talks with visibly trembling hands or while sweating profusely. Audiences tend to feel sympathy for people who seem so nervous, but that doesn't make it any easier to be the person shaking or perspiring.

Our rational selves may understand that practice will decrease our terror, but many of us still avoid practicing because it brings us into contact with unpleasant emotions. Avoiding what we fear, however, only makes us fear it more. For that reason, behavioral psychologist Patrick C. Friman advises speakers to reframe the goal of rehearsing. The goal of

3. A study that polled 813 undergraduates at a large Midwest university found that 31 percent reported fear of public speaking, 32 percent reported fear of snakes, and 34 percent reported fear of spiders. Richard W. Seim and C. Richard Spates, "The Prevalence and Comorbidity of Specific Phobias in College Students and Their Interest in Receiving Treatment," *Journal of College Student Psychotherapy* 24 (2010): 52.

rehearsing is not to eliminate fear. **The goal of rehearsing is to learn to speak while feeling afraid.**[4]

People who have performance anxiety need to rehearse because getting through a talk while nervously rehearsing it in front of friends is good preparation for getting through a talk while nervously delivering it in front of strangers. It's not just that each time we practice, we get a bit better at delivering our talks. It's that when we practice, we acquire concrete, physical experience in fear *management*. Rehearsing teaches us that we can deliver our talks and answer questions about them even while feeling fearful. I'll also repeat, because it's important, that everyone needs to rehearse, even superconfident speakers who have no performance anxiety. Confidence bolsters skill, but only practice hones it.

If you struggle with extreme anxiety when giving talks, you can, if your health care provider recommends it, take beta blockers to mute some of the physiological manifestations of nerves. Over time, whether medicated or not, the more you practice giving talks, the more likely you are to lose some of your fear. Or in the lingo of behavioral psychology, "the best way to thwart the negative reinforcement process is to stay in the presence of the stimuli" that causes it.[5] Feel the fear, speak while feeling the fear, and eventually, the fear will become less imposing. As it loses its hold over you, the fear may even dwindle.

Because the only way to overcome the fear of speaking is to speak while fearful, if you are a graduate student, I recommend

4. Friman, "Behavior Analysts to the Front!," 110.

5. Friman, "Behavior Analysts to the Front!," 110.

treating the first years of your graduate program as one long rehearsal for the talks you will start delivering during the last years of your degree and ever after. Use any occasion your program offers to practice your presentation skills: seminars, colloquiums, working groups, graduate student conferences. Don't throw those presentations together the night before. Follow the protocols in your discipline when deciding whether to deliver them from notes or from a text, and give yourself ample time to rehearse. I also recommend presenting at conferences as early in your career as possible. If you are feeling nervous about giving your first paper, you can start with conferences that are small and have a reputation for being friendly and supportive (your advisors can help you identify these). By the time you have given your first full-length invited lecture you should have had several opportunities to speak about your research in front of strangers. And even after you have become a seasoned pro, never give a talk without rehearsing it fully first.

How to Rehearse

A singing teacher of mine once said, "What you practice, you will do." If you practice by mumbling your talk at top speed while never raising your eyes from your notes, that's what you're teaching yourself to do when you actually deliver your talk. Having made the case for why you should practice, the rest of this chapter offers tips about how to do so effectively, as well as about other kinds of preparation to help your talk go smoothly.

The following advice assumes that before you rehearse, you have, as per the previous chapters, finalized an engaging, organized, and fluid outline or text. If you are using media, you have created user-friendly slides and audiovisual materials that do things that words alone cannot do as effectively. You have acquired some facility using your voice and body, and you have figured out your costume (for more on that, see chapter 9).

With that in mind, here's a rehearsal schedule.

A Few Weeks Before Your Talk

Practice delivering your talk on your own, and revise accordingly.

Read your talk aloud, straight through. If you will deliver your talk while standing, stand each time you rehearse. Time yourself and divide the number of words in your talk by the number of minutes you spent delivering it. Now you have a sense of your baseline pace. If it's faster than 130 words per minute, you need to slow down. Slower is usually better, unless you're clocking in under 110 words per minute, which might not be energetic enough for some audiences. Don't overthink this; anywhere between 110 and 130 is fine. The key is to identify your default pace so you have a way to calculate how many words you need to cut later to get your timing right (more on that below).

As you read through your talk the first time, keep a pen in hand and very quickly place a mark next to anything you may want to revise. Do not stop to rewrite anything: You are timing yourself, and you're practicing what it is like to deliver your entire talk, so you need to read it through without pausing.

Certain problems are easier to detect when delivering a talk than when drafting it—another reason to rehearse. If you're speaking from notes, rehearsals may reveal that some of your notes are too cryptic, some too detailed, some too sparse. Make your marks, and fix the problems later. Sometimes a particular idea is so challenging to express that your notes need to word it more precisely. Some ideas need to be broken down in more detail; sometimes you realize you can spend less time belaboring the obvious. Rehearsing your talk will also give you more information about where you do and don't need repetition. As noted in chapter 3, lectures require some redundancy, but you don't want too much of a good thing.

Rehearsing gives you a sense of how well your examples work off the page. You may find that a story you opened with would feel better as a conclusion. An example that felt great in writing may feel awkward when you imagine sharing it aloud with an audience.

Finally, as you rehearse, note any place where you yourself start to lose interest in what you're saying. These may be places where audiences will also find themselves drifting. Put a note next to any spots where your attention wanes and decide later whether to cut or revise them.

If you're working from a fully written text, test how your prose sounds when read aloud. Put a mark next to any sentences that cause you to run out of breath or that looked good on the page but fall flat because they lack the rhythmic flow or beat we call cadence (discussed in chapter 7). You'll have already worked at keeping your written syntax conversational (see chapter 2) and your signposting frequent and clear (see chapter 3). But inevitably, when you practice delivering your talk for real, you will find places that need tweaking. Make a note of those, go back to the drawing board, revise, read the new result aloud again, and congratulate yourself on having already logged two rehearsals.

Annotate your script. Once your script has stabilized, it's time to annotate it. Consider this a pro tip: most of the scholars I interviewed advised doing this. Develop your own system of using italics, bold, symbols, and bracketed or highlighted phrases to remind you

1. When to put slides up and take them down
2. Which words to stress by delivering them more loudly
3. Which words to stress by delivering them more softly
4. Where to raise your pitch at the end of a sentence to indicate a question
5. Where to deliver a point offhandedly
6. Where to deliver a point solemnly
7. Where to deliver a point humorously
8. Where to take a very deep breath
9. Where to slow down
10. Where to speed up
11. Where to pause for a soft stop
12. Where to pause for a full, hard stop
13. Where to ad-lib and about what
14. When and how to look at the audience (see below)
15. When to step closer to your audience or screen and when to step back

Most of these annotations are optional. You may find that you intuitively know where to introduce expressive inflections but find it more difficult, when delivering your talk, to remember to make eye contact from time to time or to slow down before describing your key finding. If so, it's perfectly legitimate to annotate your script to remind you to do these things, just as musicians annotate scores and actors annotate scripts. Not having to remember all these moves while delivering your talk ("Wait, is this where I thought it would be good to slow down?") can help you stay more present throughout your lecture.

Consider getting a director. Getting direction can be especially helpful at early career stages, when you have the least amount of experience delivering talks and teaching lecture classes. I would also recommend doing this for high-stakes talks at any career stage. You don't need a professional theater director; remember that while academic lectures are performances, academics tend to be suspicious of anything too theatrical, too showy, or too razzle-dazzle.

Your director should be a friend who is equally good at identifying strengths and pointing out weaknesses and who can offer concrete fixes for any problems they flag. If that's too tall an order for one friend to fill, find two or three. These friends do not need expertise in your topic. They're not there to focus on *what* you're saying but, rather, on *how* you're saying it—to help make sure your talk is what Daniel Immerwahr called "presentationally legible." It's great to include a few specialists in your test audience, but it's essential to enlist people who will focus less on suggesting one more article for your literature review and more on how effectively your words, slides, voice, and body are communicating your ideas and engaging your audience (as discussed in chapters 3, 6, and 7).

Practice looking at your audience. What you practice, you will do. As you rehearse, practice looking at all parts of the room. If you're new to this, start by making eye contact with your imaginary audience each time you change slides or begin a new paragraph, then graduate to making eye contact every sentence or two. When rehearsing, aim to look directly in front of you as much as possible: not at your screen, not at your notes, not at your text. If you use slides as prompts, practice glancing at them quickly on your laptop and then lifting your head to address your audience, or practice facing your audience even when pointing at slides on a screen.

If you speak from notes, use words or short phrases, not complete sentences, so that you don't have the option of reciting your notes verbatim.

Practice looking at your notes quickly to get your bearings. If your notes are handwritten, make sure they are easily legible. If they are printed, use fonts large and dark enough to be visible at a glance, and use blank spaces to separate distinct points. Train yourself not to start speaking until you are no longer looking at your notes but have lifted your head away from them and are making direct eye contact with your imagined audience.

If reading a text, never, never look down at it the entire time, no matter how many speakers you have seen do this. Rehearsing your text multiple times will help you internalize it so that you know what's coming next. That familiarity will give you a moment between sentences to make eye contact with your audience.

If reading a printout of a fully scripted text, practice holding the printout in your hand, more or less at chest

level, as an alternative to placing it on a lectern or podium or table. For a great example of how this facilitates eye contact with the audience, watch Elisheva Baumgarten's talk and note how she often held her text in her hand, with the top of the page at around shoulder level.[6] This small adjustment kept more of Baumgarten's face visible to the audience even when she was reading from her script. Because she literally had less distance to cover when raising her head from her text than if the text were lying flat on the podium, she could look up and make eye contact more often. Holding up one's notes or script also makes it easier to gesture, which makes delivery more dynamic. This method doesn't work for people whose hands shake a lot, whether from nerves or too much caffeine, and that's a lot of people. But if you can, give it a try.

When conducting dress rehearsals with your test audience, ask them to model looking tired, grumpy, bored, or zoned out because that's how most people will look during your talk, even when that's not how they feel. Academic audiences don't feel obligated to look encouraging, and most of the people in your audience will default to seeming disaffected or inadvertently hostile even though they're not. If your talk is polemical, some people may even look hostile because they are. That's okay. Remember, as noted in chapter 5, that academics express interest by arguing. It's better for your audience to be riled than to be bored.

6. Elisheva Baumgarten, "Shared Appeals to Different Gods: Jews, Christians and Medieval Prayer," Helen Diller Distinguished Annual Lecture, Center for Jewish Studies, University of California, Berkeley, February 21, 2023, posted March 11, 2023, by @Berkeley Center for Jewish Studies, YouTube video, 1:19:48, https://www.youtube.com/watch?v=904TwPbA7b0.

Use rehearsals to get comfortable making eye contact with people whose countenances are blank or even disaffected. Take a tip from David Levine and center yourself every time you make eye contact with a grump. Breathe a bit more deeply, become a bit more upright, open your chest a bit more. Your aim is not to cajole the grump into looking less crabby. You are learning to cajole *yourself* into not being unsettled by audience reactions. An open posture communicates confidence in oneself and one's audience. Never assume that your audience is antagonistic, but remember Levine's counsel that if they are, "you wrong-foot them by being open and available."

Never look at only one person for too long, even when answering a question that person posed (as noted in chapter 5). However, if you find that someone is nodding and smiling and looking supportive, you may find it helpful to make eye contact with them more often. When rehearsing in front of friends, ask one member of your test audience to look encouraging throughout the talk, and practice returning to them regularly. My very first job interview took place in a crowded hotel room with over a dozen faculty members, most of whom looked like they hadn't stepped outside for days; in some cases, they probably hadn't. They were exhausted; I was nervous. It helped to anchor my gaze to the one person in the room who smiled and nodded at almost everything I said, even though his enthusiasm was so atypical for an academic setting that I started to wonder if he was okay.

Practice your timing. Rehearsals are crucial for managing time effectively when you actually give your talk. You don't need to worry about ending a few minutes too early; this almost never happens, and when it does, nobody minds. Do be fanatical about making sure you end on time. Branden Joseph advised: "Make sure your talk stays within the allotted time. Do not go over the allotted time. There's no excuse for that and nobody likes it. Rehearse it and make sure." I've exceeded my allotted time once in my life, and it was because I hadn't rehearsed. I still feel bad about it, and I've made sure that it never happened again. We've all been there, and it always sucks, for the speaker and for the audience. It's even worse if you're presenting at a conference, as I was. The moderator held up a sign telling me I was out of time, so the only person who suffered was me, because I had to stop before getting to some of my key points. Sometimes, however, the moderator doesn't feel comfortable cutting someone off, and the person who goes over steals time from the other panelists. That's unfair to them and to the people in the audience who came to hear them.

Use your first read-throughs to determine your baseline reading rate. Use that to calculate how long your talk will take to deliver, and then, to be on the safe side, **subtract a few minutes from your allotted time so that you can be certain not to exceed it**. Speakers often find themselves going over time, which I take to be a sign that many don't fully rehearse their talks. I've heard even very distinguished speakers say, "I'm going to skip a bit here because I'm running out of time." I have seen someone show an image, tell the audience they were going to skip it because they were running out of time, immediately recount in detail what they would have said about it if they weren't skipping it—and then return to that very image later in the talk. None of that would have happened if they'd rehearsed more. Practice would have taught them that far from being expendable, this image was one of their touchstones. If you can manage to cut on the fly, more power to you, but you'll always make a better impression and show more respect for your audience by delivering a talk that fits the allotted time without last-minute, harum-scarum adjustments.

Adhering to the time limit is hardest with conference presentations that are only ten to twenty minutes long, especially if the protocol in your discipline is to speak from notes, not text. For this reason, Robert Mawhinney has graduate students in his theoretical physics group practice their talks twice before actually presenting them. In his experience, during the first practice session, most talks take *twice* their allotted time. To deliver an effective fifteen-minute presentation requires ruthlessly triaging your claims and evidence. Aim to present one and only one important finding. Illustrate that key finding by mentioning no more than three examples or data points, only one of which you discuss in depth. Be rigorous about sticking to one assertion per slide. No digressions—you'll be halfway through a charming anecdote, and then, before you know it, the moderator will be passing you a note that says "wrap up in one minute."

Timing is also a challenge when cutting down a draft of a full-length article or book chapter to fit the full-length lecture format. If you are speaking at a rate of 130 words per minute, and you've been given fifty minutes, so are aiming for forty-five, then your talk will be 5,850 words. That's shorter than most book chapters and slimmer than many articles in the social sciences and humanities. Talks work best when drafted as talks, then revised for publication. It's much more difficult to take fully polished material that is designed to be read, but hasn't yet appeared in print, and try to shoehorn that into talk format. Sometimes, however, you'll be drawing on very polished work. If it's an article or book chapter that is much longer than 5,850 words, aim to present only part of the whole. Do not try to cram in a shorter version of every point you cover; you'll end up not doing justice to any of them. Identify which claims matter most and which evidence works best. Eliminate the rest entirely or mention a few points in passing in order to plant seeds for the Q&A. Never, never, never try to cram a too-long talk into a too-short time period by reading it faster.

Some disciplines have very interactive talks, in which audience members interrupt speakers during the talk to pose questions, challenge claims, and request clarifications (I called these "disputations" in chapter 2). When rehearsing this kind of talk, you'll need to ask both the experts and the nonspecialists in your test audience to challenge you mercilessly. I've seen questions start to arrive as early as five minutes into a talk. Use rehearsals to develop what I call an accordion strategy, which enables you to compress or extend your talk to fit whatever unpredictable amount of time ends up being available. Start by identifying the shortest version of your talk you could possibly give—the elevator pitch. Prepare that ninety-second digest and rehearse that as your opening. Even if you get interrupted early on, you will have gotten your main point across. Make sure not to start with the obvious: "It is 2022, and the economy is struggling with inflation." Instead, start with the controversial proposition you aim to prove: "Central banks can fix inflation." That way you don't risk getting interrupted before introducing your key idea. In the rare event that few people interject and you have time to expand, have notes handy listing additional evidence or interesting corollaries to your main point and use those to fill the extra time.

Rehearse your talk in front of several test audiences. After running through your talk a few times on your own, for a group of friends, and in front of a director, deliver it to as mixed an audience as possible. It's best to get feedback from academics and nonacademics, specialists and nonspecialists, people in your discipline and outside it, graduate students and faculty at diverse career stages. You might ask your department to let you deliver a talk and invite colleagues from across the university, or you can volunteer to deliver your work in progress to a reading group or seminar at your home institution or nearby. If you can't achieve the necessary variety with a single test audience, muster a few audiences. The further people are from your research area, the better they will be at identifying what you have taken for granted is clear but isn't actually coming across. Sometimes this will be a point of fact; sometimes it will be about why your claims matter at all.

Whenever possible, tell your test audience or a few of the people in it (friends, close colleagues) what kind of feedback you want. It can be helpful to ask them what they thought the key takeaway was, so that you make sure it's what you want it to be. It's also useful to have them note where they felt most engaged and most checked out, so you have that guidance when revising—you never want to cut what's working. Always solicit comments about your delivery. Ask your test audience if you are audible. Request their opinions about your costume, eye contact, posture, and gestures. Query them about whether the talk felt too long or too short. If your audience dislikes something your director told you to do, listen to your audience, not your director.

You need a test audience willing to be direct and honest. If you're a graduate student, don't rely solely on what faculty advisors tell you. Many senior professors I spoke with expressed trepidation about telling students how to improve their delivery, for fear of undermining their confidence. That's an understandable and laudable concern, though I would urge faculty mentors to set it aside and give advisees tactful and specific advice. We should never tell anyone, "You have a boring voice," but we can suggest that a speaker vary their pitch to keep their audience engaged. Instead of saying, "Talk louder," focus on your experience of their practice talk and on the professional context: "It was difficult to hear you in the back, and when you're giving a talk, it's important that the whole audience can hear you."

I also recommend that students proactively ask advisors for specific feedback. Faculty advisors have usually heard graduate students speak in seminars and colloquiums and have also often observed them leading discussion sections or teaching undergraduate courses. If you as a student ask a faculty advisor, "Is there anything about how I speak, stand, or dress that I could modify?," odds are good you will get an informed, helpful answer. If you are feeling fragile (as I often did while in graduate school and even for many years after), you can ask, "What am I doing that is effective, and what could I improve?" Peers can also be a great resource for this kind of advice—fellow graduate students, when you are pursuing your doctorate, and trusted colleagues, once you become a professor.

Format your script for ease of delivery. Use a very large font so that you can see your notes or text from any distance, even if the lighting in the room is dim or you lose your reading glasses just before the talk starts.

Number your notes or pages so that if you drop them, you can reorder them quickly.

Once you have finalized your script and formatted it in a large font, insert page breaks so that you don't have to flip a page in order to complete a sentence.

Memorize the opening and closing of your talk. Speakers tend to be most nervous during the first five minutes of their presentations.[7] The more you practice your opening lines, the more fluently you can begin. The more fluently you can begin, the lower your baseline fear will be, and the better you will be set up for the rest of your talk.

Similarly, by ending confidently and fluently, you minimize jitters as you transition to fielding questions. As noted in chapter 3, audience attention is at its peak soon after you begin and soon before you end your lecture. If you memorize your opening and closing, you can make maximum eye contact with your audience when they are most fully concentrated on you.

Test your costume. As noted in the following chapter, on how to dress, before officially delivering your talk, you want to practice delivering it at least once in the outfit you'll be wearing (including the shoes). Wear your outfit for the entire day. The day of your talk is not when you want to learn that you are visibly sweating through your jacket, that your pants

7. Friman, "Behavior Analysts to the Front!," 111.

feel too tight after you have a meal, or that your footwear gives you blisters after a couple of hours.

A Few Days Before Your Talk

Prepare your tech. If you have slides, run through all the steps described in chapter 6. If you are printing out notes or a text, do so a few days before your talk, because your office printer is waiting for the moment you most need it to run out of toner or get intransigently jammed.

Get some information. If appropriate, ask your host a few days before your talk for information about the equipment in the room where you'll be presenting. Does it have a podium, lectern, microphone, projector, laptop, screen, lighting, Wi-Fi connection, laser pointer, remote clicker, and so on? Adjust your tech and plans accordingly.

Pack some snacks. Acquire and pack some portable, high-protein snacks so that you have something to eat about an hour before your talk that isn't a chocolate muffin from the campus coffee shop or a candy bar from a vending machine that will likely have you crashing halfway through your talk.

The Day of Your Talk

Prepare your body. Giving a talk is like running a marathon. When you leave your lodgings on the day of your talk, make sure to bring those high-protein snacks you were prudent enough to pack. Avoid eating very salty food, because you don't want to be too thirsty during your talk. Hydrate, but not too much, for obvious reasons. Some people find that doing aerobic exercise the morning of the day they give their talk helps them feel both calm and energized when they deliver it hours later.

Prepare the room. Whenever possible, arrive in the room at least ten minutes before your talk begins; half an hour is ideal. Figure out where you will stand. From that position, make sure you have some way to keep track of time, even though you will have already amply rehearsed your talk to make sure it is five minutes shorter than the time you were allotted. If there's no clock in the room, try to borrow someone's watch so that you don't have to wake up your phone to see the time, which may make you seem distracted.

Most importantly, before the talk begins, find someone to help you test acoustics. This can be your host, an audience member who arrived early, or someone wandering the halls. Start by asking them to stand at the front of the room and speak normally, while you go to the very back. It's important to start your test by listening, not by speaking. You need to know how a normal conversational tone carries (or doesn't) to the back of the room, because the back of the room always fills up first, and that's where it's usually hardest to hear someone standing at the front. Rooms have all kinds of acoustical quirks that you will only discover if you put yourself where your audience will be. Loud fans, street traffic, weird dead zones: get a sense of those and add intensity as needed so that people in those spots can hear you.

If there's a microphone, do the same tests with your helper using the microphone. This will help you decide if you need to use it.

Next, switch places and ask the person helping you to go to the back of the room while, with and without a microphone, you speak at a volume you can sustain for the duration of the event. Can they hear you? Great. Now plan to talk even a bit louder, because your sound won't carry as well once the room fills up.

Next, do a tech run-through. Figure out where best to place the microphone, because even if you're not planning to use it, you may decide to start doing so at some point. If necessary, connect your laptop to the projector using the dongle you were smart enough to bring with you. If you have media presentations, test them, including sound if any of your clips have sound. If you're using slides, cue up the one you want people to see when they enter the room, before your talk begins (see chapter 6). As noted in the chapter on media presentations, always have paper copies of your slides to hand so that you can still describe them even if the tech breaks down entirely—a rare but not impossible occurrence.

Just Before Your Talk Begins

Silence your devices. Silence all notifications on your laptop if you are using it, and turn off all your other devices, including your smartwatch. I once witnessed someone's watch start *talking* during their lecture.

Shut the door. Sometimes the door to the room where you are delivering your talk stays open and you find yourself competing with hallway chatter. If that happens, it's okay to pause, walk over to the door, and close it. This is something the host should do but often won't, because they're either absorbed in your talk or are concerned that getting up will seem rude or be distracting. Instead of leaving your audience in suspense about when someone, anyone, is going to get up and close that damned door, do it yourself.

And then deliver your talk with confidence and brio, secure in the knowledge that you're going to do a great job because you have practiced, practiced, practiced.

9

How to Dress

"YOU'RE GOING to have a chapter on how people should dress?" My friend, a distinguished full professor with multiple advanced degrees, waved her second glass of wine at me and opened her eyes wide. "Wow, you're brave. Better get the press's legal department to look it over. I would *never* tell anyone I worked with how to dress."

Of all the chapters in this book, this one, on how to dress to give an academic talk, has been the most controversial. Where to place it, what to say in it, whether to include it at all: Everyone's had an opinion, and few of those opinions have overlapped. There was only one opinion that everyone shared, including me: no one should ever offer unsolicited advice on a student's or colleague's appearance or clothing. "I feel like it is a Title IX violation to comment on how a student dresses," remarked one person when I asked if he ever advised grad students on how to dress for talks. He's right, and everyone I spoke with took this for granted. While it is okay for me to offer general advice about how to dress to a general reader, academia is a workplace, and at work, each of us should keep any opinions we have about an individual's appearance to ourselves—indeed, we should aim not to have any opinions about that at all.

For this very reason, the people you work with are unlikely to tell you how to dress effectively to give your academic talk. Your friends outside academia may be more forthcoming, but they also may not be the best judges of how to dress for scholarly occasions.

Why do we need this chapter? Because no one will tell you what to wear to give your talk, but people will still notice and react, often subconsciously, to your sartorial choices. In the summer of 1988, just after my first year of graduate school, I cut off my shoulder-length hair and showed up to the first day of fall classes with a buzz cut. I expected some of my professors to comment on this dramatically new look. To their credit, they did not. Crickets, until I arrived early to a seminar offered by a professor with whom I was somewhat chummy. She looked at me and said dryly, "You cut your hair." Wow, I said, you noticed—no one else has. "I think," she said, "that you should distinguish between those who noticed and those who said something to you about it. Because no one could not notice."

Exactly. Most people are noticing, even when they don't say anything about it or don't even consciously notice that they noticed. What you wear to deliver your talk matters. The same colleague who noted that advising a student about their outfit would be a potential Title IX violation remarked, "I've never been asked and I've never offered advice about what someone should wear to a job talk." After a beat, he added, "But I do hear funny stories."

I could share some of those stories, but I won't, because they're impossible to anonymize: scholars who make unusual clothing choices make a lasting impression. I defend anyone's right to wear whatever they want in any setting. But be aware that it doesn't necessarily make for a good academic talk if your clothes attract as much attention as your ideas, because that distracts from what you are saying. People get engrossed in anything surprising, and they tend to be surprised by whatever departs from norms, conventions, and expectations.

That's not the most helpful way to think about what to wear, though, because what critical thinker wouldn't want to question or resist norms, conventions, and expectations? I find it more useful to reframe the question of dress in terms of the theatrical metaphor that kept cropping up in my interviews with experts. Shifting the focus away from norms enables us to pose the question of what to wear in a new way.

What Is Your Costume?

An academic talk is a performance. **For this performance, you should don the costume of a professor.** This means that your outfit is effective if it either communicates to your audience that you are a professor or elicits no surprise or incredulity once they learn this is your trade. This can be hard for those who like to look snazzy because professors have a reputation for dressing not so well. I'm not saying you should dress badly or adhere to some banal stereotype involving tweed, elbow patches, and shapeless skirts that hit below the knee. As I note below, you must feel good in what you are wearing. So once more, with nuance: **your talk is a performance in which you play the role of *yourself as a professor*.** If you're feeling stuck about how to dress to give a talk, you can take some cues from established scholars whom you admire and with whom you identify. If you're not a mainstream person, find other scholars who aren't mainstream. If you're a bit of a dandy, find the other dandies; a bit of a hippie, find the other hippies. Don't care much about what you're wearing? You'll find plenty of models for that as well. The hope is that you can find a few sartorial touchstones no matter what your style.

By speaking of costumes, I'm not suggesting that you dress in a way that feels inauthentic. Rather, I'm suggesting that the clothes you wear when delivering talks should reflect your *work* persona, not your full, unique personality. Your work persona consists of the traits you project as a professor. Your personality makes up how you act in all situations, including private ones. Your work persona overlaps with but is not identical to your personality. If you are an especially bubbly person, your work persona might be more reserved than your personality; if you have a quiet and shy personality, your work persona might be more outgoing.

Your costume should also reflect your discipline and subfield. For example, most art historians, as befits scholars devoted to the aesthetic, tend to dress with more flair than most sociologists. Within art history, professors of contemporary art tend to dress more informally than those who study earlier periods. Scientists often deliver talks in T-shirts and shorts.

Above all, your costume **should make you feel psychologically and emotionally comfortable**. If you find yourself wondering about any aspect of your outfit, change it. You do not want to worry about skirt length or tie color or an itchy waistband while delivering your talk.

Your costume should allow you to take very deep breaths. Whatever you wear, it should be compatible with taking the long, deep breaths that chapter 7 explained are essential to delivering a talk effectively. You can still wear something tailored, even snug, if that's your preference (it's always mine). A formfitting outfit can even help you tune into your breathing by enhancing your proprioceptive awareness. The key is to make sure that whatever you wear has enough give to allow you to expand your waist, ribs, and chest when you inhale deeply and also allows you to move around easily and make expansive gestures.

Your costume should work whether you are standing or sitting, still or in motion, in full view or behind a podium. Before deciding on an outfit, try it out in a variety of positions. You won't always have information about the room setup before you give your talk (see chapter 8), and even when you do, last-minute venue changes are not uncommon. You don't want to assume you'll be standing behind a podium, invisible below the waist, only to find yourself in full view while sitting at a desk.

Wear comfortable shoes. Most talks are delivered in the afternoon or evening, and feet swell as the day progresses. Sometimes you will have to meet with people before giving your talk, then stand for almost two hours to deliver your lecture and answer questions, then attend a reception and meal. Treat your feet accordingly. Foot pain is distracting. Even if you are willing to endure it in certain situations, you'll do better if you can devote your full attention to presenting information and fielding questions. Your shoes should also be in good condition; an eminent historian who is also one of the best-dressed people I know still remembers delivering a talk wearing one shoe that had a hole in it and feeling her attention mildly diverted by that the entire time she spoke.

Test your outfit for a full day, and solicit honest opinions about it at your dress rehearsal. Never give a talk in an outfit you have tried on only at the store. You need to experience how it shrinks or wrinkles or expands, how it feels against your skin, and how it responds to your movements and to changes in your body temperature. Wear it for a day, out of the house, and test whether it makes you feel comfortable, strong, and aligned with your work persona. Do solicit other people's opinions. As noted in chapter 5, we all have a friend/colleague/frenemy who blurts out what other people are often thinking but are too tactful to say. Invite the blurter to your practice talk. If your tie looks silly or your suit needs altering so that you don't look like a gangly teenager about to attend their cousin's wedding—or, to quote feedback I once got during one of my dress rehearsals, if the bow circling the waist of your jacket makes you look like a present about to be unwrapped—the blurter won't keep that to themselves. Their tactlessness at the dress rehearsal will help you determine whether you want to modify anything about your costume for the main event.

Select a costume that travels well. Most of us deliver talks away from our home institutions and have to pack our costumes in small suitcases. Make sure your costume doesn't wrinkle a lot when folded and can be easily freshened up by being exposed briefly to the steam that lingers after you run a hot shower. Some of you may love wielding a hot iron, but don't count on having access to one.

Bring a backup costume. Avoid wearing your costume in transit, because accidents happen: drinks spill, pens explode, fabric tears. If possible, pack a backup costume in case of wardrobe malfunction. If you're the indecisive type and options unnerve you, make your backup costume as similar to your primary outfit as possible, if not an outright duplicate. Finally, buy a miniature sewing kit and always pack it in your travel bag, along with some spare buttons.

10

Delivering Your Talk Virtually

DELIVERING A TALK over Zoom or other videoconferencing platforms has many advantages.[1] Cutting down on travel can be a boon for the environment, departmental budgets, and speakers' packed schedules. Virtual talks (delivered only over Zoom) and hybrid talks (simultaneously live and over Zoom) can attract people who would not make it to talks in person. Shy speakers may find it easier to deliver talks online, and timid audience members may find it easier to ask questions via the chat, which also enables moderators to filter, combine, and prioritize questions.

When it is good, a Zoom talk can be very, very good, even more intimate and accessible than a live one. Slides are often more visible when each audience member can view them on a personal device. Seeing speakers amid books and plants humanizes them. Participants can access flawed but still helpful

1. Zoom is not the only videoconferencing platform, but it is the one that has become shorthand for videoconferencing in general. I use "Zoom," therefore, as I might refer to xeroxing even when making copies on a Ricoh or Epson machine.

live transcripts, and recorded talks usually include captions that can easily be translated into multiple languages.

When it is bad, a Zoom talk is horrid—and many Zoom talks are memorably, even comically bad. Poor setups can make presentations difficult to see and hear, and broadcasting from home can be a recipe for distraction. A cat wanders in and settles down on the speaker's lap, showing off its ability to make better eye contact with the audience than the speaker themselves. Then the cat jumps up and leaps across the speaker's desk, loudly knocking a glass of water to the floor. A neighbor's dog yaps. Washing machines churn and beep. Jackhammers drill. Doorbells chime. The ill child the speaker stayed home to care for (hence the Zoom talk) urgently needs attention.

The speaker who avoids domestic brouhaha by delivering a Zoom talk from their work office may find their computer amplifying noise from the hallway, from neighboring offices, and from an impromptu live concert on the campus green. Avoid those issues by donning noise-canceling headphones, and not only do you look like you are flying a plane instead of giving a talk, but oh wait, you're frozen, because the Bluetooth connection causes lags, and whoops!—halfway through the talk, the headphones lose their charge.[2] Even speakers who have avoided all of the above by hunkering down in a hotel room (usually because of a canceled or delayed flight) often end up speaking with a bed visible in the

2. In 2025, Zoom offered an option for suppressing background noise: https://support.zoom.com/hc/en/article?id=zm_kb&sysparm_article=KB0059985.

background and getting interrupted when cleaning staff try to enter the room.

Other common issues conspire to degrade the quality of Zoom talks. The speaker is backlit. The speaker is too brightly lit. The speaker delivers their talk looking down, to the side, at the ceiling. The speaker is so close to the camera that the audience can't see the speaker's hands but does notice each time the speaker glimpses their own image on-screen and fleetingly pats their hair or adjusts their tie. The audience has a distractingly close view of the speaker's eyes darting from left to right while reading. Let's not even talk about nose hair. Though everyone in the audience has been on the other side of this and knows how hard it is to sustain eye contact with the camera, those watching can't help but feel disengaged when the speaker seems to be looking everywhere but at the viewers.

It's hard for academics to give excellent Zoom talks because doing so requires being trained to perform for the camera, and academics are not professional actors. Even professional actors rarely perform for a fixed laptop camera; they perform for mobile cameras operated by expert cinematographers receiving guidance from professional directors. To be sure, we've all seen videos online made by amateurs using iPhones or laptops who don't seem to have any trouble looking at the camera. What's their secret? I've watched many videos that explain just that, and it turns out that those people aren't really amateurs. They've filmed themselves in specially designed spaces, deploying a raft of external equipment, and have spent hours training themselves to look comfortable on-screen—hours most academics cannot spare.

COVID-19 lockdowns sent academics flocking to Zoom, which by April 2020 had 300 million users.[3] Since then, many departments have decided to make invited lectures into hybrid events simultaneously delivered live and on Zoom, though more recently, the tendency has been to return to exclusively live talks. It has also become common to record live, Zoom, and hybrid talks and share those recordings with department members, with people who registered for the event, or with the general public, usually via YouTube. Not all speakers want to make their presentations available beyond the specific place and time of the talk. **Hosts must have your permission to share or post your talk online and should ask for that well in advance of your talk.** You have every right to refuse permission, especially if the plan is to make the recording available to an unrestricted audience. If you're a younger scholar and feel uncomfortable saying no, Branden Joseph recommended telling your host that you need to consult with your advisor or publisher and then getting them to back you up.

If you are willing to consider having your talk posted online, add a clause to any agreement you sign stating that you reserve permission until you've seen exactly what will be posted. Make sure to keep a copy of the amended version and to draw your host's attention to your codicil well before you deliver your talk. Now your host has an incentive to make an

3. That figure comes from Mary Whitfill Roeloffs, "Want to Make a Good Impression on Your Zoom Call?," *Forbes*, September 27, 2023. The same article notes that by April 2022, Microsoft Teams, another videoconferencing platform, had 270 million users.

adequate recording. I've seen excellent recordings done with very basic equipment. I've also seen terrible recordings where I couldn't hear the speaker or see their slides but had a great view of the backs of the heads of audience members fidgeting, chatting, and checking things on their brightly lit phones. It's not the end of the world, but speakers should have the final say in how they're presented to the public. For hybrid talks that take place simultaneously in person and over Zoom, the temptation is simply to hit record within the Zoom platform itself and then post that recording. That is the cheapest and easiest way to record a Zoom talk. It is not the best way. In fact, it is the worst. Why? Because what makes for an effective presentation in person usually creates a crappy presentation on Zoom.

This brings us to the core of this chapter: how to give a good academic talk on Zoom.

Most of the techniques presented elsewhere in this book also apply to talks delivered on Zoom: engage the audience, explain ideas clearly but not reductively, offer road maps, put very little text on your slides, speak clearly and slowly, rehearse, think about your costume.

Live and virtual presentations do, however, differ in ways that this chapter addresses. In person, speakers can glance frequently at their slides and notes and should gesture broadly, move around a bit, and shift their gaze to look at everyone in the room. Do that on Zoom, and you will look like a distracted clown. Okay, you say, then just have the live speaker do in person what works well on Zoom. Unfortunately, what works on Zoom, as we will see, is to stay very still; keep your hands close to your body, even when gesturing; and fix your eyes on one spot for at least 80 percent of your presentation. Do that in person, and you will look like a catatonic mummy.

In other words, it's physically impossible to connect effectively with an in-person audience and a Zoom audience at the same time. That's why hosts who want to record your hybrid talk should use an external camera and film you live, not use the recording generated by the computer camera transmitting you to the virtual audience. This doesn't require expensive equipment. The external camera can be a phone mounted on a tripod at least ten feet from the speaker.[4]

4. For examples of excellent recorded talks, done with a variety of equipment, I recommend Leslie B. Vosshall, "Bitten: Why Are Some People More Attractive to Mosquitoes than Others?," NIH Director's Wednesday Afternoon Lecture Series, National Institutes of Health, October 26, 2022, posted October 28, 2022, by @NIH VideoCast, YouTube video, 1:00:10, https://www.youtube.com/watch?v=XNUlwMfqClg; Elisheva Baumgarten, "Shared Appeals to Different Gods: Jews, Christians and Medieval Prayer," Helen Diller Distinguished Annual Lecture, Center for Jewish Studies, University of California, Berkeley, February 21, 2023, posted March 11, 2023, by @Berkeley Center for Jewish Studies, YouTube video, 1:19:48, https://www.youtube.com/watch?v=904TwPbA7b0; Suzanne Marchand, "Herodotus Versus the Higher Criticism: George Rawlinson, Anglican Historian and Translator," Oxford Antiquity Conference, September 30, 2022, posted November 22, 2022, by @Faculty of Classics, University of Oxford, YouTube video, 47:21, https://www.youtube.com/watch?v=kmGjNuEJOyg; and Bathsheba Demuth, "Do Whales Judge Us? Interspecies History and Ethics," Environment Forum, Mahindra Humanities Center, Harvard University, November 6, 2019, posted December 5, 2019, by @Harvard University, YouTube video, 1:51:47, https://www.youtube.com/watch?v=yh_kJA0Naug. If you are the speaker and are being recorded, I recommend against taking notes while you speak. This reads fine for those attending the talk in person but can appear surprisingly dismissive or disengaged on-screen. Finally, I found that it worked much better on-screen when introducers spoke extemporaneously and addressed the camera directly. If you are introducing a speaker and find it impossible to memorize the precise titles of their

Having explained why in a hybrid setting it works best to focus on your live audience and be recorded by an external camera, the rest of this chapter focuses on how to give a good talk delivered *exclusively* via videoconferencing: how to manage your equipment, your space, your appearance, and your audience. Giving a good virtual talk requires a lot of preparation, so I've organized this chapter as a timetable that starts one month before your virtual talk and concludes thirty minutes before your virtual meeting begins. If you have given lots of Zoom presentations, you'll be familiar with a lot of what follows, but you will probably also find some novel suggestions worth considering. I've watched many Zoom talks, and there's always something that even experienced presenters could improve. If you've never done any of the things this chapter describes, you can, if necessary, execute most of them in a few concentrated hours. But if you have more time, the following is an efficacious way to parcel out your prep.

Four Weeks Before Your Virtual Talk

Practice using the videoconferencing platform. If you are new to the platform you'll be using, or know only the rudiments, or have used it often but rarely as a presenter, make time four weeks before your talk to explore it. Schedule some meetings where you are the only participant. During these solo practice meetings, familiarize yourself with as many

---

key publications, refer to them more synoptically (X has written articles on A, B, C), which also has the advantage of being more engaging.

functions as possible—not only the basics, such as screen sharing, but features like the built-in laser pointer and whiteboard. Click on every option visible on the screen. It's a great way to learn the platform's affordances and to build muscle memory when it comes to executing the most common steps. If, like me, you tend to think that the computer is out to get you, it's also great to discover that nothing terrible will happen if you click the wrong button—you'll just figure out how to get back to where you need to be.

If you need help understanding how to use Zoom, Microsoft Teams, or Google Meet, those companies offer detailed support and instructions, and the internet runneth over with material explaining how to use them. I sifted through many of those videos and blog posts to research this chapter. If you are using Zoom, I recommend Shrot Katewa's "How to Give a Presentation on Zoom?," which clearly explains, verbally and visually, how to use basic functions and more advanced ones.[5]

Obtain access to a professional Zoom account. During the COVID-19 pandemic, when many academics began to use Zoom, everyone accepted that presentations might be suboptimal. That is still the case if you are delivering your talk online due to an unexpected emergency. But if there is no crisis, people now expect virtual presentations to be more seamless and professional.

5. Shrot Katewa, "How to Give a Presentation on Zoom?," Art of Presentations, February 24, 2023, https://artofpresentations.com/how-to-give-a-presentation-on-zoom/.

To deliver a talk on Zoom effectively, you need to schedule a meeting that lasts longer than forty minutes, so either you or your host must have access to a Zoom account that won't automatically end the Zoom meeting halfway through your talk. Before paying for this, see if your institution provides free or low-cost access to a professional subscription.

Make sure your computer and Wi-Fi network can support your virtual presentation. You will need a computer with rapid processing speed (check online for the latest figures). Ideally, you will connect that computer to the internet using a wired connection (like an ethernet cable) rather than a wireless one. I know, I know, an ethernet cable, what is this, the 1980s? You probably don't have an ethernet connection at home, but ask an IT person at work whether you can access one on campus, because having installed ethernet back in the day, few campuses ever bothered to remove it. In 2024, every videoconferencing article I read recommended using an ethernet connection. Ethernet guarantees you will be able to deliver your talk even if you can't connect to Wi-Fi—as happened to me once when I had to give a talk at 4 AM my time to an audience in a very different time zone and found myself unable to access campus Wi-Fi. Everyone who could have helped me was asleep. I was able to troubleshoot by turning my phone into a personal hotspot for my laptop, but that isn't always an option.

Ethernet also provides a strong, stable connection that means the dreaded "Your connection is unstable" message will never flash across your screen. An unstable connection can make your voice start to crack up and slow down, which will make you sound like you actually are in the 1980s—like Prince at the beginning of the album version of his hit song "1999" but less cool. Connecting via ethernet will also prevent your image from freezing during your talk, usually at a moment when your eyes are closed and your mouth is open and often before *you* get the message that your connection is poor. (If this happens, stop your video and switch to audio only, which takes up less bandwidth than video and can better survive a poor connection.)

If you are using a wireless connection, make sure that your Wi-Fi speed is at least six hundred kilobits per second; 2.5 megabits per second is recommended, and between four and five megabits is ideal. There are websites that enable you to test Wi-Fi speed; before using them, do some research to see if people currently consider them secure.

Your Wi-Fi will work better if you position your computer close to the router. That's not always possible. Your router may be in a closet, and while spaces filled with soft fabric are great for reducing echoes, you probably don't want to deliver your talk from a closet.

When using Wi-Fi, make sure to dedicate all available bandwidth to your Zoom talk. During your practice sessions, get used to the following drill. Exit any applications you will not be using in your presentation. Disconnect all your other devices from Wi-Fi. Ask everyone in your household to stay off Wi-Fi for the duration of your Zoom session. This way, if you experience connection problems, you know the issue lies with your setup.

If you have trouble with your Wi-Fi connection during your practice Zoom sessions, consider buying a range extender. If you give many talks at home, it may be worth upgrading to faster Wi-Fi.

Having done all this prep work, conduct another practice session that includes screen-sharing AV materials; as I explain further along, AV materials are not as optional in Zoom talks as they are in live talks. At this stage, you may not have your talk completely done, and that's fine. The AV materials you practice with don't have to be the exact ones you'll use in your talk, just similar media types. If you're going to be working with Keynote, use an old Keynote presentation or throw one together that has at least eighteen slides because, as we'll see, virtual presentations require more slides than live ones. If you're going to be playing sound files or video clips, include these in your practice presentation to confirm that you have sufficient processing and Wi-Fi speed to support every component of your talk.

Three Weeks Before Your Virtual Talk

You've practiced using your videoconferencing platform, obtained access to an account type that won't time you out, ascertained that your hardware and software are up to spec, and conducted practice sessions that include screen-sharing slides and media. Now it's time to set up your space.

Test acoustics. You already determined how close you to need to be to your router to maintain a good Wi-Fi connection (if you can't connect via ethernet). Within those bounds, start identifying where it would be best to give your talk.

Start with acoustics. Avoid large and relatively empty rooms, which will make your voice echo. Virtual presentations sound best in smaller rooms filled with books and furniture, especially softer furniture upholstered in fabric or leather.

Carpets and rugs reduce echoes and make your voice sound warmer.

When giving a presentation that with Q&A may run close to ninety minutes, it helps to be in a room whose temperature you can control. If that requires running a noisy heater, fan, or air conditioner, or speaking with the window open, find a space whose heating or cooling produces less fracas.

Assess potential interruptions. Identify a space that will be as free from external noise as possible. Possible noise sources include household appliances, household members (including pets), neighbors, workplace colleagues, and hotel staff. Are you delivering your virtual talk from a campus office that often has people gathering right outside your door who engage in loud conversations while they wait for the elevator, the restroom, and faculty in neighboring offices? My campus office has all of the above, plus a vent that is basically a hole in the wall between my office and the office next door. My neighboring colleague is quiet, but many of the students who stop by his office are very, very loud. When I give a virtual talk from my office, I get out my Sharpie and put a sign on my door that reads, in large, dark letters, "Quiet Please / Zoom Talk in Progress / Do Not Knock." Sometimes that works. If I were giving a high-stakes talk, I'd research access to a campus recording studio designed to block out external sounds.

If delivering your talk from a hotel, you won't be able to alter your space much, but you can stop by the front desk and let them know exactly when you will be in your room on a work call. Ask for their help making sure you don't get interrupted. Just before your talk, check to see if any cleaning staff are on your floor. If they are, explain your situation and ask them not to enter your room during your talk—as I've sometimes seen happen. If that does happen, I think it's best to excuse yourself for a moment, then mute your audio and stop your video while you talk with the staff.

This is a lot to keep track of—but it all matters. In a 2022 study, industrial design researchers asked a group of twenty people aged nineteen to fifty-six drawn from diverse professions, including academia, to provide detailed feedback on their experiences with Zoom meetings. Those participants remembered even small interferences to their Zoom meetings long after they had taken place and identified them as distracting, disruptive, and sometimes even distressing.[6]

Establish your background. Most people place themselves in front of a wall, but it can also work well to position yourself in front of a corner where two walls meet. Keep some distance between you and whatever is behind you. Experts have found that, when videoconferencing, a speaker's background makes a stronger impression on viewers than a speaker's clothing and that the most congenial backgrounds are spare but not bare, "familiar but not too busy."[7] A study analyzing 167 reactions to still images from videoconferencing calls

6. Minha Lee, Wonyoung Park, Sunok Lee, and Sangsu Lee, "Distracting Moments in Videoconferencing: A Look Back at the Pandemic Period," in *Proceedings of the 2022 CHI Conference on Human Factors in Computing Systems*, edited by Simone Barbosa, Cliff Lampe, Caroline Appert, David A. Shamma, Steven Druck, Julie Williamson, and Koji Yatani (New York: Association for Computing Machinery, 2022), 1–21.

7. See Roeloffs, "Want to Make a Good Impression on Your Zoom Call?"; and Briar Goldberg, "7 Zoom Mistakes You Might Still Be Making," Ideas.Ted.Com, February 9, 2021, https://ideas.ted.com/7-zoom-mistakes-you-might-still-be-making-and-how-to-raise-your-video-skills/.

found that houseplants and bookshelves (or the two combined) made the best impressions.[8] If you're delivering your virtual talk in a hotel room, do your best to make sure there are no beds, couches, or kitchen appliances visible behind you.

Backgrounds should personalize the speaker, but not too much. If you have books in your background, try to be far enough away from them that your virtual audience won't get distracted reading the titles on their spines. Posters on walls and tchotchkes on shelves are fine, but don't quirk out too much. I didn't know whether to groan or laugh when I saw a professor whose field was *not* music deliver his Zoom talk in an office containing a very large electric guitar. I regularly have Zoom meetings in front of a bookcase that used to hold a pink polyester "Pepper" handbag. Who is Pepper, you might ask? Pepper was a doll popular in the 1960s, and the handbag pictures her in a teal swing coat, strolling with two fetching black dachshunds on leashes. (Google it—or you know, maybe, just don't.) I find my Pepper handbag campy and evocative, but no one I work with ever needs to see this object. When I realized that it was visible in my Zoom backdrop, I moved it.

I advise against virtual backgrounds. They create a gooey halo that becomes especially noticeable and off-putting when you make even the tiniest motion.[9] Participants will find it

8. Cited in Roeloffs, "Want to Make a Good Impression on Your Zoom Call?"

9. See Brian Watkins and Miguel Ramlatchan, "Zoom Conferencing Best Practices for Professional Presentations, Conferences, and Events," in *Instructional Message Design, vol. 2*, ed. Miguel Ramlatchan and Casey Kohler (Old Dominion University Digital Commons, 2022), 373, https://digitalcommons.odu.edu/instructional_message_design_vol2/14/.

easier to connect with you if they can place you in three-dimensional space.

If you do use a virtual background, keep in mind that you still need to make your actual space ready for prime time. Should Zoom automatically log you out (which sometimes happens, even to pros), your actual background will probably be exposed to all when you log back in.

Two Weeks Before Your Virtual Talk

Position your equipment. You will need a surface ample enough to comfortably fit your computer and any peripherals: mouse, notes, glass of water, other devices you may be using. You will also need to be close enough to an outlet or power strip that, with the help of an extension cord, you can keep your computer charged during the entire talk.

Once you have placed your computer on this surface, plug it in and get ready to start making the most crucial adjustment needed to give a good virtual talk: **aligning your eyes with your computer's camera**. The camera is the audience's eye.[10] Your Zoom audience sees what your computer lens sees. If you're looking at your audience members on your screen, you are *not* making eye contact with them. You are making eye contact with their images on your screen. **To make eye contact with audience members you must look at your camera.** This is crucial, so I'll repeat it. The image of audience members on your screen is just that: a picture. Only when

10. Gartner-Schmidt, "New Normal," 25S.

looking at your camera are you making eye contact with your audience.

Where is the camera? You'll need to research that for your particular computer. On my MacBook, the camera is right next to the small dot at the very top of my computer screen, so I'm going to refer to the place where you need to direct your gaze as "the dot." On a Zoom call, if you look at someone's image on your screen instead of looking at the dot, that person will not see you looking at them. That person will see you looking down because on your screen their image lies *below* the dot. Looking at a person's image on your screen during a Zoom call is like looking at someone's feet while talking to them in real life. Don't talk to the feet.

Test this for yourself. Ask friends to participate in a practice Zoom meeting. Start the meeting, opt for gallery view and a visible self-view, and hit "record." Keep your self-view on for now. Take a photograph of the screen so later you can remember where each friend was positioned in the gallery view.

While recording, look at each friend's image on the screen and say hi to them, one by one, naming each friend as you greet them: "Now I am looking at your image, X, on the screen." Next, briefly look at yourself, fleetingly touch your hair or face, as people almost always do when they glimpse themselves on Zoom, and say, "I just glanced at my image on the screen." Finally, find the dot next to your computer camera, look at that, and say, "Now I am looking at the dot next to the camera." Keep talking to your friends *while looking only at the dot*. Periodically repeat, "I am still looking at the camera."

To test your peripheral vision, keep recording while looking at the dot, and, without glancing down at the screen, ask your friends to make some movements. Each of them can hold up a finger or two, raise a hand, wave, smile, or shrug. While continuing to focus on the dot, state whenever you notice them move and what you think they are doing. This will give you a sense of how much information your peripheral vision provides, which varies from person to person.

Review the recording and see what you look like when doing the things you narrate. You'll see that you address viewers most directly when you say that you are looking at the dot. You'll probably also see that you seem kind of weird while talking to the dot, because you're addressing a dot instead of a person (an issue I address later in this chapter).

If you're having trouble finding the dot or staying focused on it, take a small Post-it and fold it in half. Cut a semicircle out of the center, at the fold. Open the Post-it. Voilà! It now contains an open circle. Place the Post-it on your computer, sticky side down, so that the open circle frames the dot. The Post-it makes it easier to focus on the correct spot.

Now it's time **to position your computer, desk, and chair so that your eyes easily align with the camera on your screen**. Typically, if you sit in a chair facing a laptop computer placed on a desk or table, you are set up to type. Your hands are not in the same place as your face, so the computer camera will be significantly below eye level. To align your eyes with the computer camera you will need to adjust the heights of your computer, chair, and/or desk. The exact heights will depend on your dimensions and those of your furniture. The key is to adjust these heights by small increments. If the adjusted chair height makes it difficult for you to plant your feet firmly on the floor, rest your feet on footrests, yoga blocks, books, or firm pillows. Avoid dangling feet—pressing your feet lightly on a stable surface will conserve your energy and help you maintain optimal posture throughout your talk.

The cheapest way to adjust your laptop computer's height is to stack it on books, which conveniently come in many sizes. The *best* way to adjust your computer's height is to be able to raise and lower your table and chair. Small adjustable-height tables are available at fairly low cost (and can double as standing desks). Adjustable chairs can be more expensive, but you can often find used ones on sale. I recommend using an adjustable chair that does not roll, swivel, or pivot, because it's important to stay still while speaking on Zoom. Why? First, even small movements trigger your camera to shift its autofocus, which compromises the quality of your image. Second, people's brains are wired to detect and respond to movement, and even small movements can distract your audience. Some viewers may even feel dizzy or nauseated when someone on-screen rocks toward and away from the camera. It's easy, when caught up in giving a talk, to rock and roll without realizing it, so best to sit in a chair that stays planted in one spot.

If you are using a laptop, I recommend placing it on an adjustable stand and the stand itself on your desk or on a stack of books. Adjustable laptop stands have lips to keep your computer from falling and grippy feet to keep the stand itself from sliding around. Many stands also allow you to angle your camera slightly up or down, which can make you look better on-screen.

To determine whether your eyes align with the camera, you need to test how you appear on-screen. Open up Photo Booth, take some stills, adjust. Expect this process to take a while—

when I do it, it often requires fiddling for half an hour. It's not enjoyable, but it's time well spent. Having established the basic position of your computer and chair using still photos, start recording a solo Zoom meeting to see if you are looking directly at the camera when you think you are.

Having placed your camera at the optimal height, so that your eyes align with the camera, it's time to center your body in the frame. You're aiming for a tight medium shot that captures you from the shoulders up. Start a practice Zoom call and adjust the distance between your chair and your desk until you see your head in the middle of the screen, with ample room above it. The bottom of the frame should roughly correspond with the bottom of your shoulders. Keep in mind that you need to be within two feet of the computer for its microphone to capture your sound effectively; for most people, that will correspond to the distance the computer needs to be at for a medium shot.

Once you've set all this up, note down the exact height of your computer, table, and chair and the exact distance between your computer and your chair—as in, get a tape measure and write down information about every element you had to adjust. If you can, take a tip from people who work on stage and film sets and use painter's tape to block out where your chair, table, and computer stand need to be relative to one another. This will save you from having to start this process over from scratch if a household member borrows your adjustable chair or your cat knocks down that stack of books on your desk. (Just to be clear, I love cats.)

Set up your lighting. Having established your backdrop and positioned your table, chair, and computer stand, it's time to set up your lighting. **Always place your light source *behind* your computer camera, *facing* you, and shining directly on your face.** Never deliver a virtual talk with a window behind you; you will be backlit and difficult to see. Avoid being lit from above or the side, unless you are trying to look like a Hollywood film star circa 1940 (in which case you will need at least three lights).

It's best not to face an uncovered window. Exposed windows provide strong but variable lighting, and computer cameras react very strongly to even small changes in light. When the sun is shining, you may be overly lit, washed out, and hard to see. When clouds cover the sun, your face will suddenly grow dim. I recommend delivering your talk in a room that either has window coverings or does not get direct sunlight.

A tall standing lamp is the ideal lighting source. Place the lamp behind your computer, facing you. The best lamps for videoconferencing purposes are dimmable, lightweight, and stable. Even if you don't give many virtual talks, I recommend purchasing a low-cost ring light, designed for use with computer and phone cameras. A ring light is a circular bulb mounted on an adjustable-height pole that sits on a tripod. The circular bulb provides even lighting, the adjustable-height pole allows you to train that light on your face, and the tripod provides a stable base. Dimmers and the ability to choose between warm and cool lighting modes are reasonably priced features that make it easier to optimize the lighting for your particular coloring and features. If you don't want to get a ring light, use a tall standing household lamp; ones with flexible goosenecks work well. In a pinch, a clip-on utility lamp works if you have something to secure it to and can angle the lamp so that the bulb shines directly on your face. Computer cameras are designed to work best with white lightbulbs; look for ones marked "daylight" or "neutral white," in the 5,000–6,500 Kelvin range and between 800 and 1,100 lumens: less and your image will be grainy, more and the lighting may be too harsh. If using multiple light sources, do not mix warm and cool lights.[11]

Practice your bodily comportment. Make sure your chair position enables you to access your written or printed notes and that you can easily reach your keyboard to start screen sharing, advance your slides, or use your virtual pointer. As noted earlier, it's best not to sway or rock when delivering a Zoom talk, so practice speaking while sitting in a chair that doesn't roll, swivel, or pivot. Perching on a barstool and standing are also options, but potentially uncomfortable ones, especially for longer presentations. See what works best for you. Remember that proximity to the camera makes even tiny motions loom large, so try to keep your hands still when you aren't intentionally gesturing. Twiddling your thumbs or fiddling with rings or necklaces in view of the camera will pull focus from your presentation.

If all of this sounds unnatural, it is. The art of seeming natural on camera requires managing one's body in artificial ways.

Now that you've committed to being weirdly immobile, it's time to complicate things by setting yourself up to sit energetically. Engage your core and plant your feet with your knees far

11. For the science on this, see Joong Nam Yang and Steven K. Shevell, "Surface Color Perception Under Two Illuminants: The Second Illuminant Reduces Color Constancy," *Journal of Vision* 3, no. 5 (2003): 369–79.

apart.[12] Remember that your knees won't be visible on camera because your setup cuts you off at the shoulders. Now lift your upper body. You want your torso open and expanded to help your voice sound resonant and warm, which matters even when you have a computer microphone to amplify you.

I haven't suggested that you "sit up straight," because you shouldn't be perfectly upright. Having planted your feet and lifted your torso, you will achieve the most flattering and sustainable angle if you scoot back very slightly in your chair and lean a tiny bit forward.[13]

Having established your overall posture, it's time to practice making gestures that are visible within the camera frame. Set up a practice Zoom meeting so you can observe yourself and develop a sense of where to place your hands to make your gestures visible on-screen. Your range of motion will probably be smaller than it would be in person, and you'll likely keep your hands closer to your torso and your elbows farther out and slightly farther back than you usually do.[14]

Set up your screen for your talk. You've probably already started wondering about a Zoom talk conundrum. I've stressed how important it is to look at the camera. If you're looking at your slides, notes, or script, then you're not looking at the camera, and few of us can deliver a forty-five-minute or

12. For more on how to sit effectively while speaking, see Lauren Sergy, "Should You Stand or Sit When Presenting on Video Conference?," posted February 2, 2021, YouTube video, 6:16, https://www.youtube.com/watch?v=zsuKYgvP9WQ.

13. See this video, which includes many useful tips: Katie Fehlinger, "How to Look Good on Zoom," posted December 1, 2020, YouTube video, 11:25, https://www.youtube.com/watch?v=RIJVIXI8jHY.

14. See Fehlinger, "How to Look Good on Zoom."

even ten-minute talk without looking at slides or notes, and some of us are in disciplines whose protocols require reading a fully prepared text. Therein lies the rub. If you're looking at the camera, you can't see the materials you need to see to give your talk. If you're looking at the materials you need to see to give your talk, you're alienating your audience by not looking at the camera.

The solution: **minimize the audience's view of you during most of your virtual presentation and show slides throughout your talk so that viewers do not focus on your face**. Why minimize the audience's view of you? Let's consider what the audience will see if you keep your speaker view maximized. They will see your eyes constantly shifting from left to right as you read your slides, notes, or script. They will see you looking up, down, and to the side, everywhere but at the audience, as you consult your notes, look at your slides, or read your text. They will see you smiling too broadly, crinkling your eyes, frowning and furrowing your brow, and maybe even spitting a little. All of this will be magnified because you are sitting very close to the camera and viewers are sitting very close to their computers. If you're not showing slides, your image probably occupies each audience member's entire screen. In real life, you're always at least several feet away from even the people in the front row. In a virtual presentation, you are literally in everyone's face. You could be a movie star and this still wouldn't be a good look.[15]

Here's what I recommend. Memorize the first two or three sentences of your talk, and deliver them slide-free while

15. See Gartner-Schmidt, "New Normal," 24S–25S.

looking directly at the camera. Then, after those first three sentences, start screen sharing a slideshow that will be up for the duration of your talk. Research shows that audiences prefer to see presenter and content simultaneously, so, even though a good talk resembles a podcast (see chapter 6), I don't recommend making yourself invisible during virtual presentations.[16] Instead, as soon as you start showing slides, **minimize your image so that it appears in a small box**. You've already seen an example of this, in Figure 3 in chapter 4, in the screenshot from Barbara Henry's talk on Russian literary underworlds.[17]

Once you start your slideshow and put your image in a box, you enter what Microsoft Teams calls "Standout Mode," because your slides stand out as the focal point.[18] You can move the box containing your image to different points on your screen. I prefer the bottom right-hand corner, but experiment with what you like best. You can control the box size by clicking on the minimize icon and then clicking and dragging the box corners. I recommend keeping the box small enough

16. Watkins and Ramlatchan, "Zoom Conferencing Best Practices for Professional Presentations, Conferences, and Events," 367.

17. Barbara Henry, "Road, River, and Book: The Russian Literary Underworld," Sawchen Lecture Series in Slavic Studies, Department of Central, Eastern, and Northern European Studies, University of British Columbia, and Bicentennial Speaker Series, 2020–21, North American Dostoevsky Society, January 26, 2021, posted March 19, 2021, by @North American Dostoevsky Society, YouTube video, 54:09, https://www.youtube.com/watch?v=utjsnbRq2HM.

18. There's also a side-by-side view where speaker and slides take up equal space, but I don't recommend it—the speaker is large enough for disconcerting eye movements and glances away from the camera to be highly visible, and the essential slides, crammed into a much smaller space, are less legible.

to make it difficult for viewers to see your eye movements (which take up a fraction of your image) but large enough for them to easily take in your whole face at a glance. Get your practice audience to help you figure out the best sizing across variations in computer setups.

Don't keep yourself in a small box for the entirety of your presentation. Identify a few moments in your talk that are easy for you to deliver while looking directly at the camera, such as transitions from one section to another. At those moments, toggle out of "share screen" and briefly return to taking up the entire screen so that you can reconnect with the audience for around thirty seconds before going back into your box.

If you're giving a short ten-minute presentation as part of a panel, I recommend creating Assertion-Evidence slides (see chapter 6) that serve as prompts. Use these slides instead of notes or text to deliver your entire talk directly to the camera. The brevity of the assertions allows you to glance down briefly at each slide to remind yourself of the assertion before returning to making eye contact with the camera while you explain your evidence. For those who prefer very precise instructions, you can achieve a good balance between looking directly at the camera and consulting your notes or slides if you glance down for about one second every thirty seconds.[19]

The advice to fill your screen with slides for all but the first and last seconds of your virtual talk may seem to contradict a rule presented in chapter 6: never use slides to do what words alone can do. There is no contradiction. Words alone cannot

19. Julie Hansen, *Look Me in the Eye: Using Video to Build Relationships with Customers, Partners and Teams* (Denver, CO: Acting for Sales, LLC, 2021).

overcome the rules of the physical universe—the rules that make it impossible for you, as presenter, to look straight at your camera while also looking at your screen. Your videoconferencing slideshow therefore *is* doing something that words alone cannot. It is occupying your audience's attention so that they do not focus on your eyes darting around as you look at your notes, slides, and text.

What kinds of slides should you use during a virtual talk? For talks that focus on the presentation of complex data, use the same slides you would use in a live talk, plus "filler" images depicting relevant material. If your slides contain hyperlinks, remember that while those work when you're in PowerPoint and Keynote, they may not work when you share your screen on Zoom. If that's the case, either create a separate slide that shows the material that the hyperlink would take you to or plan to share the actual site within a browser.

For talks that focus on the close analysis of images, use the same slides you would use in a live talk and add some filler slides. You need filler slides because once you have stopped analyzing a particular piece of visual evidence, you should remove it from view. Filler images can portray relevant people, places, and things. If your talk closely analyzes texts, you can create filler images of authors, book covers, and original editions or show paintings, prints, and photographs that evoke when and where the text was written. For talks that focus on the close analysis of audio materials (usually music), consider filler slides that depict composers, performers, specific performances, and performance venues. When showing video, click "Optimize for Video." When sharing computer sound, make sure to share your sound as well as your screen and to optimize your audio by selecting "stereo."

Always have basic information about your filler images ready to hand and be ready to say something about each of them. To keep your audience focused on your talk, keep your filler images simple. Follow the advice offered in chapter 6 about using images as visual wallpaper. Atmospheric images should reinforce your claims without drawing attention to themselves, like a film soundtrack that emphasizes the mood established by the script and the actors.

Some technical notes about showing slides while on Zoom. Many people embed notes in their PowerPoint or Keynote that then guide their presentations. But when sharing slides on Zoom, you don't want to share your notes (your audience will get distracted reading them). You have options here. One is to share only a portion of your screen in Zoom and exclude the notes on your slides from your viewers' field of vision. I don't recommend this, because the notes on your screen will be quite small and hard for *you* to read, but you can test that for yourself. Another option is to separate your notes and slides by using a second device to display your notes to yourself.[20] A third option is to write or print out your notes, outline, or text and place the pages (numbered, of course) on a stand next to your laptop. Mount that stand on some books so that the middle of each page aligns with your computer camera.

20. For instructions on how to do this (from someone who has not properly aligned himself with the camera recording him, offering excellent evidence of why that matters), see Dave Paradi, "Using PowerPoint Presenter View in a Zoom Meeting on a Mac with 2 Screens," posted July 24, 2021, by @ThinkOutsideTheSlide.com, YouTube video, 4:52, https://www.youtube.com/watch?v=3RX-JyUss8s.

(Luckily most academics will have easy access to the very large number of books needed to set up a good Zoom talk.)

Your Zoom talk is done and it's time for the Q&A. If you haven't already done this to deliver your final lines, remember to stop screen sharing and to maximize your view for speakers. It's common with virtual talks for moderators to collect questions in the chat. If possible, instead of peering into the chat yourself, ask the moderator to read questions aloud, so that you can maintain eye contact with your audience. If your audience is visible and in gallery view, adjust your settings to pin each speaker and move the part of your screen showing pinned speakers as close to your computer camera as possible. That way, when you answer a question, you can address the dot while still having a peripheral view of the questioner. From your practice sessions, you'll have learned that your peripheral vision gives you more information than you think it does. Remember, people will feel you are looking at them precisely because you are looking at the dot next to your camera and *not* at their image on your screen.

When answering questions, take care not to look up, as we often do when thinking aloud.[21] I do this all the time, though I have no idea who I think is up there. Practice thinking while looking at the camera and keeping your head level with the dot.

Here's a final piece of next-level advice about addressing the camera that you might play with during the rehearsals

21. See Brandt Krueger, "The Art of Maintaining Eye Contact with the Camera," *Event Tech Podcast*, December 20, 2021, https://helloendless.com/eye-contact-with-the-camera/.

described in the next section. While you speak to the dot or the Post-it at the top of your screen, imagine that you are looking at a person you know well and enjoy talking to about ideas. Mentally project that person's image onto the dot. If you can, imagine them smiling and nodding as you speak. Julie Hansen, in a nonscholarly guide I found helpful, offers detailed advice on how to do this.[22] I've tried it, and though I'm no actor, I found it transformative. When I imagine that I'm looking at a congenial, enthusiastic colleague, smiling and nodding at me, I feel my face become more mobile and expressive. When the dot is just a dot, I feel my face become rigid and inert. I look like a machine because I am talking to a machine (and a very tiny one, at that). The changes are visible in my practice recordings. If this kind of visualization comes easily to you, picture your imaginary dot-sized friend looking curious when you pose a question, surprised when you say something counterintuitive, and amused when you make a joke. Or not—there's enough to keep track of already.

A Week or So Before Your Virtual Lecture

Rehearse your virtual lecture, including your AV materials. Remember the mantra of chapter 8: practice, practice, practice. With just a week to go before delivering your talk, it's time to rehearse within your videoconferencing platform itself. Practice looking directly at the camera without consulting any notes during the first and last minute of your talk. Get comfortable with common maneuvers: toggling in and out of

22. Hansen, *Look Me in the Eye.*

screen sharing; minimizing, moving, and resizing your speaker view; and moving through your AV materials while screen sharing. Familiarize yourself with Zoom's whiteboard and laser pointer features and with animating and annotating slides within Zoom.[23] Answer pretend questions while looking directly at the camera, following all the tips in the previous section.

Record each rehearsal, then play the recordings. It's tempting to focus on how you look. Don't. Focus on what your audience will focus on: your slides and your voice. Coordinate your remarks with your slides, and aim to change slides every few minutes or whenever you change topics, whichever is more frequent. When watching each recorded rehearsal, identify what you are doing well and identify the two most important things to tweak. Make those two adjustments in your next rehearsal. All this rehearsing takes time but will pay off handsomely when you give your actual talk.

Finally, do a dress rehearsal with a live audience of a few friends joining the call. Start by asking them to describe what they see and hear, so that you know from the start if your setup needs any adjustment. Then record your full talk and a prac-

23. For instructions on how to animate and annotate slides in Zoom, see Carmen Simon, "3 Science-Backed Techniques to Hold Your Audience's Attention on Zoom," *Digital Selling* (blog), February 9, 2023, Corporate Visions, https://corporatevisions.com/blog/3-science-backed-techniques-to-hold-your-audiences-attention-on-zoom/; and Sarah Ohnigian, Jeremy B. Richards, Derek L. Monette, and David H. Roberts, "Optimized Remote Learning: Leveraging Zoom to Develop and Implement Successful Education Sessions," *Journal of Medical Education and Curricular Development* 8 (2021): 1–4. For how to use a Zoom laser pointer, see https://21stcenturyav.com/screen-sharing-during-video-calls/; for how to use a Zoom whiteboard, see Ohnigian et al., "Optimized Remote Learning."

tice Q&A session without stopping. When you're done, keep recording and ask for feedback. Later you can share your recorded dress rehearsal with trusted advisors who can't attend and ask them for additional feedback.

When rehearsing, pay attention to your vocal delivery. This chapter has focused a lot on how your presentation looks, but managing your voice matters enormously in a virtual talk because your voice will be more prominent than your image. Keep in mind that computers can distort sound, as well as the likelihood that some audience members will be in noisy settings while listening to you.[24] It's also the case that many people report being easily distracted when watching a virtual talk. To compensate for all this, use more pauses, speak more slowly, and articulate more crisply and precisely than you would in a live talk.[25] Don't, however, speak louder than you normally would—that helps in a live talk but can be counterproductive in a virtual one.

In at least one recorded rehearsal, wear the outfit in which you plan to deliver your talk. Make sure your clothing contrasts with your background so that you don't blend into the wall. Warm, monochromatic tones work best; avoid anything too bright or too dark. Opt for solid colors as well, because pinstripes can flutter on-screen, and complex patterns can strobe. Avoid anything that might cast a glare: shiny fabrics and watches, tie clips, lustrous jewelry. It's also good to avoid

24. "Videoconferencing is highly dependent on sound" (Lee et al., "Distracting Moments in Videoconferencing," 18). Gartner-Schmidt similarly notes in "The New Normal" that on Zoom, voice takes the place that body language does when speaking to a live audience (25S).

25. Gartner-Schmidt, "New Normal," 25S, 27S.

dangling, clanging accessories that might create distracting movements and sounds.[26] Head to toe, your outfit should be what you would wear to give a talk live. You may feel cozier wearing a blazer over sweatpants and fuzzy slippers, but you never know when you'll have to stand up on short notice, giving everyone a view of your UGGs.

Test your speaker and microphone. "Top Tips to Improve Audio Quality in Your Zoom Meetings," a 2020 resource from Stanford's IT department, offers some good tips about how to do this.[27] Ask a friend to attend a brief practice meeting to confirm that participants can hear you clearly and that you are coming through neither too soft nor too loud. Record this brief practice meeting and confirm that it is capturing you and the participants clearly. During the talk itself, if your audio is acting up, mute yourself and click on the ^ sign next to the mute button and then select "audio options."

The following is a checklist of items to cover with your host about a week in advance of your virtual presentation.

Will the talk be password-protected and invitation-only? These security measures are now standard, but they require that your host give people adequate lead time to register for your talk. I recommend, where feasible, sending your host a short guest list about a month in advance. Two weeks before your talk, ask people on that list if they've received invitations to register. If they haven't, politely let your host know

26. Watkins and Ramlatchan, "Zoom Conferencing Best Practices for Professional Presentations, Conferences, and Events," 375.

27. "Top Tips to Improve Audio Quality in Your Zoom Meetings," University IT Newsroom, Stanford University, December 7, 2020, https://uit.stanford.edu/news/top-tips-improve-audio-quality-your-zoom-meetings.

that the people on your guest list haven't yet received an invitation.

Who will host the meeting? The host should be in charge of admitting registered guests, starting the recording, making sure everyone but you is muted during your talk, handling any technical issues that arise during the meeting, and moderating the chat during the Q&A. This is too much for you to juggle while also delivering your lecture, so if the answer to the question of who will host is "no one," it's okay to request some support. If the department can't afford to hire campus IT, then they can identify a staff person whose job description includes helping with events, pay a student to host, or identify a senior faculty member willing and able to volunteer.

Ask to be made a cohost of the meeting. That way, if you happen to know how to fix a problem more quickly than the official host, you have the option of doing so.

Two to Three Days Before Your Virtual Talk

Update all the software on your computer. After updating, make sure that the updates haven't blocked Zoom's access to your microphone and/or camera. You can find instructions on how to do this online that include explanations of how to automatically adjust your microphone and suppress background noise.

Identify a backup device in case your computer suddenly fails. This is unlikely, but it's also unlikely that someone would steal your computer while you go through airport security, and that happened to a colleague of mine just before he was scheduled to deliver a talk in China. It's even more unlikely that you would drop your laptop from a seven-foot ladder during a Zoom call, but that happened to me during a nonwork Zoom call that involved installing floor-to-ceiling drapes. During the six weeks it took to get my hard drive replaced, I often had to use Zoom for work. Luckily, I had a battered old laptop to fall back on; it was missing a few keys, but it got the job done.

A backup device can be an old computer (so long as it can run the most recent version of Zoom), a tablet (but note that camera placement on tablets makes it almost impossible to center yourself on-screen), or your phone. When setting up your backup device a few days before your talk, make it sure it has the latest versions of the software that you use for videoconferencing, documents, and AV presentations. I always email myself all the components of my talk (Word files, Keynote presentations, handouts) to create a backup that I can access from any device, so long as I have the needed passwords to hand. I also email those files to my host.

The Day Before Your Virtual Talk

Temporarily disable all screen savers. Just in case you didn't do that properly, make sure your screen saver is something you're okay having a professional audience see.

Adjust your power-saving settings to make sure your device stays on for the duration of your talk. It's unlikely it will go into sleep mode while Zoom is in use, but it's also worth making certain of that.

Silence all computer alerts and notifications (audio and visual). It's not enough to exit all the applications open on your computer, though you should do that, too. Why silence notifications for applications you've exited? Because during the talk, especially during the Q&A, you may want to open your email or go to a site to find material relevant to your talk. If you haven't silenced your notifications (or disabled them altogether), then the second you open your email, the notifications will start streaming in. Ping. Ping. Ping. Oh, look, that visual preview banner is telling everyone about the coffee beans you ordered. Oh look, there's another; now everyone can see a link to that article your sister really wants you to read.

Put your phone on airplane mode, so that it doesn't weaken your Wi-Fi signal and because most phones are synced up in some way with our computers. Ditto your smartwatch and any peripherals you won't be using during the talk, like a printer. You don't want these devices waking up during your talk and providing unintended diversions.

Assume that at some point, people may obtain a fleeting view of your home screen. That glimpse might become a nice long stare at any thumbnail images and all of your file and folder names. Remove anything you would not want published on the front page of the *New York Times*. I recommend temporarily putting all folders not relevant to your talk in a larger folder marked "Desktop" or something similarly bland.

Thirty to Forty-Five Minutes Before Your Attendees Enter the Meeting

Do a tech run. Arrange with your host to start the meeting early so you can do your tech run *before* it's time to start admitting guests or recording the event.

Here's a checklist for tech runs:

- Have your host or tech support person test how the live audio sounds to participants.[28]
- Do a short test recording: On the recording, are you audible? Are the slides visible? Are you positioned properly both when in full view and when placed in a small box in the corner of the AV presentation?
- Make your mouse cursor larger and heavier than usual so that it will be more visible to your online audience. You can also turn your mouse into a laser pointer within Zoom.[29]
- If you are on a panel with multiple speakers, take a few minutes to make sure the speakers are aligned. Each should appear to be roughly the same distance from the screen, so some may have to move closer or farther from their computers. Work out how people's names and other information appear on-screen. This may vary with individual preferences, but each panelist should confirm that their Zoom name identifies them properly and corresponds to how they want audience members to address them. If you don't want to be addressed as

28. See "Top Tips to Improve Audio Quality in Your Zoom Meetings" for detailed instructions on how to test audio.

29. See Clara Nellist, "How to Use a Laser Pointer in Zoom," posted May 19, 2020, by @Dr Clara Nellist, YouTube video, 3:43, https://www.youtube.com/watch?v=wGDLCQz2qJ4, for detailed instructions on how to turn your mouse into a laser pointer.

"Dad" or "Sheila's iPhone," when your name is Eric, click on "Rename" and fill in the essential information.

- If you are moderating a lecture or presenting as part of a panel, either turn off your video or model active, attentive listening if you choose to stay visible when other people are speaking. If you are typing or looking things up in other applications during presentations, which I have seen happen more than once, everyone in the audience can see that.
- Adjust settings so that you are pinned for all participants. **Audience members for an academic talk should not have the option of choosing a "gallery" view.** In gallery view, everyone in the audience can see up to a dozen other audience members on the screen, and some people won't know how to change this. When this happens, everyone watching can see what each audience member is doing throughout the talk. This might include watching an audience member carry his computer around his house for forty-five minutes. I only saw that happen once, but it was unforgettable. The gallery view can work well for the Q&A if the audience is small, but in those cases, ask the host to activate gallery view only once the Q&A begins.

This chapter has offered very comprehensive advice because when it comes to Zoom talks, the devil is in the details. It takes a lot to make a Zoom talk work, but consider the time, energy, and carbon emissions saved by not spending hours in transit. Delivering your talk virtually enables you to reach people all over the world who might not otherwise have the chance to hear and respond to your ideas. So find that ethernet cable, incentivize anyone you live with to leave the house or stay mum for two hours, try to get your dog and cat to take a nap, and go forth and prosper.

Conclusion

I DESIGNED this book to make anyone's talks better, whether that person is, as I once was, a tongue-tied novice prone to stage fright or, as I am now, a seasoned professional who remains interested in improving my own delivery and in finding resources I can recommend to students.

In closing, I'd like to turn to the future and make two recommendations that go beyond the scope of this book.

The first recommendation has to do with research. Research on teaching and learning, especially in lecture courses, has obvious relevance to research on academic talks. It's equally obvious that there are important differences between academic talks and teaching. For this reason, it would be helpful to have more studies focused specifically on academic presentations: both the shorter talks common at conferences and the longer talks professors usually deliver solo.

The second recommendation has to do with teaching at both undergraduate and graduate levels. In the nineteenth and early twentieth centuries, elocution was part of the curriculum, and many colleges and universities had departments of rhetoric or speech that trained students in public speaking. By the 1960s, those departments had become much less common. Some of their material became the subject matter of specialized disciplines such as communications, speech pathology, and theater. Some of it migrated to extracurricular activities like debate teams or spoken-word performance. In the process, courses in public speaking fell by the wayside.

Most universities today see it as their responsibility to teach students how to write, often requiring that every undergraduate take a course in composition. By contrast, it's the rare institution of higher learning today that requires students to take courses that teach them how to speak. At many universities, credit-bearing classes in public speaking aren't even an option. Graduate students in many disciplines lack formal training in how to talk about their research, though some disciplines are better than others when it comes to creating opportunities to practice these skills informally.

I think this needs to change. For the past fifteen years, I've made oral presentations a significant part of every smaller undergraduate class I teach. Doing so taught me that students need as much support when it comes to learning how to give a good talk as they do when it comes to learning how to write a good paper. The guidelines I developed to help my students outline, rehearse, and deliver their presentations helped inspire me to write this book, because I saw what a difference they made.

Graduate students would also benefit from more formal training in giving talks. I've witnessed firsthand how graduate students thrive when they take workshops on how to write a dissertation prospectus, apply successfully for grants and jobs, and submit their research for publication. I believe we'd see similarly positive results if we created courses and workshops on how to give good academic talks. Many law schools, business schools, and divinity schools currently provide this kind of training, geared toward the specific needs of their respective professions. Those classes might offer helpful models for departments and graduate schools interested in launching pilot programs. Imagine a semester-long course where each chapter of this book defined a weekly topic. Where needed, instructors could bring in expert guest speakers to help students improve their slide design or vocal delivery. In the final weeks of the course, students could give practice talks and get constructive, formal feedback on what they are doing well and what they could improve.

I'll end, then, as I began, with the question colleagues often asked when I told them I was writing this book: Are you going to tell people how to make their talks less bad? I have, and I hope that this book has something to offer everyone who wants to give better talks and feel better about delivering them. I also hope that this book is the first of many steps in a collective, organized effort to make one of the least visible aspects of academia's hidden curriculum readily accessible to all.

LIST OF TALKS CONSULTED

1. Alessandri, Mariana. "Seeing Ourselves Through Dark Moods." Talks at Google. June 9, 2023. Posted June 9, 2023, by @Talks at Google. YouTube video, 47:11. https://www.youtube.com/watch?v=ib21lMQiwe8.
2. Allen, Chadwick. "Earthworks Rising: Mound Building in Native Art & Literature." Simpson Center for the Humanities, University of Washington. Fall 2019. Posted December 30, 2019, by @Simpson Center. YouTube video, 52:21. https://www.youtube.com/watch?v=u6LCVTB0rNM.
3. Balbale, Abigail Krasner. "The Wolf King: Ibn Mardanīsh and the Construction of Power in al-Andalus." New York University Abu Dhabi Institute. March 30, 2023. Posted March 30, 2023, by @NYUAD Institute. YouTube video, 59:31. https://www.youtube.com/watch?v=Z-TXXiz7ZTk.
4. Baron, Jaimie. "Countering Culture: Shirley Clarke and the Edges of Cinema." Radcliffe Institute for Advanced Study at Harvard University. March 29, 2023. Posted April 6, 2023, by @Harvard Radcliffe Institute. YouTube video, 59:19. https://www.youtube.com/watch?v=YUqEnb6HkUE.

5. Bassani-Sternberg, Michal. "Antigen Discovery for Development of Personalized Cancer Vaccines." Koch Institute Symposium 2023, Koch Institute for Integrative Cancer Research, MIT. June 23, 2023. Posted July 12, 2023, by @KochInstituteMIT. YouTube video, 1:04:25. https://www.youtube.com/watch?v=0GMl1G4M-0o.
6. Baumgarten, Elisheva. "Shared Appeals to Different Gods: Jews, Christians and Medieval Prayer." Helen Diller Distinguished Annual Lecture, Center for Jewish Studies, University of California, Berkeley. February 21, 2023. Posted March 11, 2023, by @Berkeley Center for Jewish Studies. YouTube video, 1:19:48. https://www.youtube.com/watch?v=904TwPbA7b0.
7. Blau, Helen. "Regenerating and Rejuvenating Aged Tissues by Targeting a Gerozyme." NIH Director's Wednesday Afternoon Lecture Series, National Institutes of Health. February 1, 2023. Posted February 6, 2023, by @NIH VideoCast. YouTube video, 1:02:48. https://www.youtube.com/watch?v=rPVoQesTplU.
8. Boynton, Susan. "Pictures Worth a Thousand Sounds." Sacher Lecture 2021, John J. Cali School of Music. February 10, 2021. Posted February 10, 2021, by @Jed Leshowitz Recital Hall at Cali School of Music. YouTube video, 45:03. https://www.youtube.com/watch?v=gkh55UTFPyI.
9. Brecht, Michael. "Blood Is Thicker than Water." Joint Seminars in Neuroscience Lecture, 2021 Winter Series, Brain Research Institute, University of California,

Los Angeles. January 12, 2021. Posted January 12, 2021, by @BRI UCLA. YouTube video, 1:05:39. https://www.youtube.com/watch?v=q4W5WcuJjsA.

10. Cha, J. Mijin. "Just Transition or Just a Transition?: The Importance of Power, Organizing, and Framing in Decarbonization." Society of Fellows and Heyman Center for the Humanities, Columbia University. April 25, 2023. Posted April 27, 2023, by @SOFHeyman. YouTube video, 1:06:49. https://www.youtube.com/watch?v=bO1KlU0ovJQ.
11. Chander, Manu Samriti. "Failed Kinship and the Brown Commons." Society of Fellows and Heyman Center for the Humanities, Columbia University. April 6, 2023.
12. Chetty, Raj. "The Economic Impacts of COVID-19: Real-Time Evidence from Private Sector Data." Bendheim Center for Finance, Princeton University. June 17, 2020. Posted June 17, 2020, by @Princeton Economics. YouTube video, 1:19:07. https://www.youtube.com/watch?v=ip5pz7gOSwI.
13. Crawford, Neta C. "The Pentagon, Climate Change, and War." Environment Forum, Mahindra Humanities Center, Harvard University. September 29, 2022. Posted October 12, 2022, by @Mahindra Humanities Center. YouTube video, 1:26:54. https://www.youtube.com/watch?v=FvFiSr7T0bs.
14. Cremer, Paul S. "Can Transition Metal Cations Be Electrostatically Screened Away from Biomembrane Interfaces?" Bent Lecture, Department of Chemistry, Columbia University. April 3, 2025.

15. Davis, Muriam Haleh. "The 'Failures' of Liberal Capitalism and the Racial Regime of Religion in Late Colonial Algeria." Society of Fellows and Heyman Center for the Humanities, Columbia University. March 9, 2023. Posted March 24, 2023, by @SOFHeyman. YouTube video, 1:18:09. https://youtube.com/watch?v=64OnyV1h6Oo.
16. Demuth, Bathsheba. "Do Whales Judge Us? Interspecies History and Ethics." Environment Forum, Mahindra Humanities Center, Harvard University. November 6, 2019. Posted December 5, 2019, by @HarvardUniversity. YouTube video, 1:51:47. https://www.youtube.com/watch?v=yh_kJA0Naug.
17. Ferdinand, Malcolm. "Writing in the Toxic Ruins of Colonial Slavery." Maison Française, Columbia University. February 7, 2023.
18. Fischer, Brodwyn. "Intimate Inequalities." Radcliffe Institute for Advanced Study at Harvard University. September 26, 2022. Posted March 31, 2023, by @HarvardRadcliffeInstitute. YouTube video, 59:51. https://www.youtube.com/watch?v=0TGMm6LASrU.
19. Gopinath, Gita. "The Power and Perils of the 'Artificial Hand': Considering AI Through the Ideas of Adam Smith." University of Glasgow. June 5, 2023. IMF Videos video, 1:04:41. https://www.imf.org/en/News/Articles/2023/06/05/sp060523-fdmd-ai-adamsmith.
20. Haynes, Annabelle E. "Towards a Poetics of Underdevelopment: Cartographies of Expropriation in Brand

and Kincaid." Department of English and Department of African American and African Diaspora Studies Speaker Series, Columbia University. January 31, 2024.

21. Henry, Barbara. "Road, River, and Book: The Russian Literary Underworld." Sawchen Lecture Series in Slavic Studies, Department of Central, Eastern, and Northern European Studies, University of British Columbia, and Bicentennial Speaker Series, 2020–21, North American Dostoevsky Society. January 26, 2021. Posted March 19, 2021, by @North American Dostoevsky Society. YouTube video, 54:09. https://www.youtube.com/watch?v=utjsnbRq2HM.
22. Henry, Zoë L. "The Kinesthetic Turn: Ruth Page, Jessie Redmon Fauset, and the Machinery of Dance Modernism." Department of English, Columbia University. January 22, 2024.
23. Herfeld, Catherine. "Thick Concepts in Economics." Conceptual Engineering Online Seminar Series. June 7, 2022. Posted June 15, 2022, by @Conceptual Engineering. YouTube video, 1:08:28. https://www.youtube.com/watch?v=UyJD8xeoIDs.
24. Hudson, Renee. "Retconning Revolution and the Solidarity of Form." Department of English, Columbia University. January 17, 2023.
25. Jacks, Tyler. "Toward Improved Cancer Vaccines: Lessons from Preclinical Models." Koch Institute Symposium 2023, Koch Institute for Integrative Cancer Research, MIT. June 23, 2023. Posted July 12, 2023, by @KochInstituteMIT. YouTube video, 1:04:25. https://www.youtube.com/watch?v=0GMl1G4M-0o.

26. Jackson, Shannon. "Ecological Time in Time-Based Media Art." Environment Forum, Mahindra Humanities Center, Harvard University. February 17, 2022. Posted February 28, 2022, by @Mahindra Humanities Center. YouTube video, 1:17:20. https://www.youtube.com/watch?v=bkUP8bdwoaU.

27. Kang, Gagandeep. "Access to Vaccines Without and with a Pandemic: Lessons from India." Mailman School of Public Health, Columbia University. April 19, 2023. Posted April 19, 2023, by @Columbia Public Health. YouTube video, 1:26:35. https://www.youtube.com/watch?v=c_e5ockYkOU.

28. Katz, Ethan. "The Mothers, the Mamzers, and the Rabbis: Reconstructing Family and Community in Post-Holocaust Jewish Law." Center for the Study of Religion, University of California, Berkeley. May 8, 2023. Posted May 9, 2023, by @Berkeley Center for Jewish Studies. YouTube video, 1:09:05. https://www.youtube.com/watch?v=iht5WIA9vSU.

29. Klitzman, Robert, Rosanne Raso, Leigh Ann McMahon, David N. Hoffman, and Danisha Jenkins. "Promising Approaches to Moral Distress Among Nurses." Panel, Bioethics Program and School of Nursing, Columbia University. June 30, 2022. Posted June 30, 2022, by @Columbia SPS. YouTube video, 1:30:39. https://www.youtube.com/watch?v=w-0A9qpej1c&t=2s.

30. Koerner, Joseph. "Dürer's Mobility." 2021 Linbury Lecture, National Gallery. January 14, 2022. Posted March 7, 2022, by @The National Gallery. YouTube

video, 1:34:52. https://www.youtube.com/watch?v=FqsCni1i9AY.

31. Kuipers, Giselinde. "Beauty as Taste and Duty: Value and Privilege in the 21st-Century Beauty Regime." Culture and Social Analysis Workshop, Department of Sociology, Harvard University. October 10, 2023.
32. Larson, Daniel R. "Understanding Transcription and Splicing Heterogeneity in Cancer Progression." Koch Institute Symposium 2017, Koch Institute for Integrative Cancer Research, MIT. June 16, 2017. Posted July 8, 2017, by @KochInstituteMIT. YouTube video, 26:28. https://www.youtube.com/watch?v=7yHmB_yXBFE.
33. Lin, Dayu. "The Neural Substrates for Aggression." Federation of European Neuroscience Societies Hertie Winter School 2018 on Neural Control of Instinctive and Innate Behaviour, Obergurgl, Austria, January 6–12, 2019. Posted April 27, 2021, by @FENS. YouTube video, 42:44. https://www.youtube.com/watch?v=fZkHshEIp3s.
34. Lofton, Kathryn. "Sensitive People: On Being Alive Today." Institute for Religion, Culture and Public Life, Columbia University. September 18, 2023.
35. Ma, John. "Polis: The Greek City-State 800 BC–AD 600." Stanford University. April 14, 2011. Posted May 25, 2011, by @Stanford. YouTube video, 1:19:34. https://www.youtube.com/watch?v=IEvv1PvVTA0.
36. Maini, Philip. "Squirrels, Turing and Excitability—Mathematical Modelling in Biology, Ecology and Medicine." Oxford Mathematics Public Lecture,

Mathematical Institute, University of Oxford. May 27, 2020. Posted May 27, 2020, by @Oxford Mathematics. YouTube video, 1:05:51. https://www.youtube.com/watch?v=H-GnVgLS4pM.

37. Mann, Catherine L. "Facing Challenges of Returning Inflation to Target: Global, Domestic, Post-COVID, Long-Term." Economics Department, Columbia University. March 30, 2022.
38. Marchand, Suzanne. "Herodotus Versus the Higher Criticism: George Rawlinson, Anglican Historian and Translator." Oxford Antiquity Conference. September 30, 2022. Posted November 22, 2022, by @Faculty of Classics, University of Oxford. YouTube video, 47:21. https://www.youtube.com/watch?v=kmGjNuEJOyg.
39. Mateos, David Moreno. "Restoring Ecosystems in a Time of Ongoing Global Change." Harvard Museum of Natural History, Harvard University. March 23, 2022. Posted November 15, 2022, by @Harvard Museum of Natural History. YouTube video, 48:59. https://www.youtube.com/watch?v=11IX5MmneI0.
40. Mbah, Ndubueze L. "Abolition Forgery: A History of the Afterlives of Slavery." Radcliffe Institute for Advanced Study at Harvard University. April 18, 2023. Posted April 18, 2023, by @Harvard Radcliffe Institute. YouTube video, 1:05:00. https://www.youtube.com/watch?v=mWJA-5V8iWU.
41. Michor, Franziska. "Computational Models of Cancer." Koch Institute Symposium 2017, Koch Institute for Integrative Cancer Research, MIT. June 16, 2017.

Posted July 8, 2017, by @KochInstituteMIT. YouTube video, 20:36. https://www.youtube.com/watch?v=rqtYLg8OZ8I.

42. Nugent, Carlos. "Imagining Land and Latinidad in the Wake of the California Gold Rush." Department of English and Comparative Literature, Columbia University. January 31, 2023.
43. Oh, Seung Hee. "Race and Gender in Heaven and Hell." Harvard Art Museums, Harvard University. May 24, 2022. Posted December 2, 2022, by @Harvard Art Museums. YouTube video, 35:53. https://www.youtube.com/watch?v=JDQzTy7dE1g.
44. Ohlmeyer, Jane. "Ireland, Empire, and the Early Modern World." Trinity College Dublin and Society of Fellows and Heyman Center for the Humanities, Columbia University. April 21, 2022. Posted May 17, 2022, by @SOFHeyman. YouTube video, 1:03:24. https://www.youtube.com/watch?v=Q_a4q03po_k.
45. Pugh, Allison. "The Stratification of Human Contact: The Present and Future of Connective Labour." 2022/2023 Distinguished Speaker Series, Department of Sociology, University of British Columbia. September 6, 2022. https://sociology.ubc.ca/news/watch-dr-allison-pughs-distinguished-speaker-lecture/.
46. Rodrik, Dani. "Where Did Globalization Go Wrong, and How Can We Fix It?" Office of the Vice Provost for Advancements in Learning, Harvard University. May 22, 2023. Posted May 22, 2023, by @Harvard - Office of the VPAL. YouTube video, 59:41. https://www.youtube.com/watch?v=fxv5RbjPLdY&t=1s.

47. Rush, Cynthia. "Six Years of Information Theory, Probability, and Statistical Learning." Yale Institute for Foundations of Data Science, Yale University. April 26, 2024. Posted June 5, 2024, by @Yale FDS (Foundations of Data Science). YouTube video, 30:43. https://www.youtube.com/watch?v=vT6qfk8bgaY.
48. Sanford, Melanie. "New Strategies for the C-H Functionalization of Aliphatic Amines." Center for Selective C-H Functionalization Virtual Symposium, National Science Foundation. July 28, 2015. Posted December 3, 2015, by @Center for Selective C-H Functionalization. YouTube video, 28:08. https://www.youtube.com/watch?v=fFC4WuSbXdQ.
49. Smith, Sophie. "The Nature of Politics." Quentin Skinner Lecture and Symposium, Centre for Research in the Arts, Social Sciences and Humanities, Cambridge University. June 9, 2017. Posted June 15, 2017, by @CRASSH Cambridge. YouTube video, 1:04:09. https://www.youtube.com/watch?v=si9iG-093aY.
50. Sorek, Rotem. "The Immune System of Bacteria: Beyond CRISPR." NIH Director's Wednesday Afternoon Lecture Series, National Institutes of Health. January 25, 2023. Posted January 30, 2023, by @NIH VideoCast. YouTube video, 1:03:07. https://www.youtube.com/watch?v=_COeBSfG53g.
51. van Dijk, Winnie. "What Can Linked Administrative Data Sets Teach Us About Eviction and Poverty in America?" Social Science Research Council. August 24, 2023. Streamed live August 24, 2023, by @Social Science Research Council. YouTube video,

1:02:30. https://www.youtube.com/watch?v=K6MfM8NLlps.

52. Vardi, Moshe Y. "Efficiency, Resilience, and Artificial Intelligence." Computer Science/Discrete Mathematics Seminar, Institute for Advanced Study. March 24, 2025. Posted March 24, 2025, by @Institute for Advanced Study. YouTube video, 1:13:57. https://www.youtube.com/watch?v=Ji84f7eLxpU.
53. Vosshall, Leslie B. "Bitten: Why Are Some People More Attractive to Mosquitoes than Others?" NIH Director's Wednesday Afternoon Lecture Series, National Institutes of Health. October 26, 2022. Posted October 28, 2022, by @NIH VideoCast. YouTube video, 1:00:10. https://www.youtube.com/watch?v=XNUlwMfqClg.
54. Waldinger, Robert. "The Good Life." Lee Kum Sheung Center for Health and Happiness, T. H. Chan School for Public Health, Harvard University. February 27, 2023. Posted February 28, 2023, by @Lee Kum Sheung Center for Health and Happiness. YouTube video, 1:02:27. https://www.youtube.com/watch?v=HUHowWFJNBg.
55. Warner, Marina. "Strangers in a Strange Land: Displacement, Sanctuary, and the Traveling Tale." Edward W. Said Memorial Lecture, Society of Fellows and Heyman Center for the Humanities, Columbia University. October 6, 2022. Posted October 14, 2022, by @SOFHeyman. YouTube video, 1:08:32. https://www.youtube.com/watch?v=aYzhzxh9eFc.

56. Wenzel, Jennifer. "Between Petro-Magic and the Pedestrian." Environment Forum, Mahindra Humanities Center, Harvard University. October 20, 2021. Posted November 2, 2021, by @Mahindra Humanities Center. YouTube video, 42:59. https://www.youtube.com/watch?v=V5RfI9vAwyI.
57. Wherry, Frederick. "Of Things Not Seen." Kinder Institute for Urban Research, Rice University. June 16, 2021. Posted June 16, 2024, by @Kinder Institute for Urban Research. YouTube video, 1:11:27. https://www.youtube.com/watch?v=QV0setHmSyE.
58. Willet, Rebecca. "Learning Low-Rank Functions with Neural Networks." Yale Institute for Foundations of Data Science, Yale University. April 26, 2024. Posted June 5, 2024, by @Yale FDS (Foundations of Data Science). YouTube video, 36:15. https://www.youtube.com/watch?v=VpTJEmoMqJw.
59. Zamora, Omaris. "Ciguapa Unbound: Blackness, Gender, and Transnational Geographies of Marronage." Department of English and Comparative Literature, Columbia University. February 6, 2023.
60. Ziegler, Tamar. "Sign Patterns of the Möbius Function." Mathematics, Physics & Computer Science Series, Masaryk University, Brno. October 10, 2024. Posted March 13, 2025, by @Muni Seminar Series. YouTube video, 55:35. https://www.youtube.com/watch?v=krTUFq8-z-U.

ACKNOWLEDGMENTS

I LOVE giving advice and take it as a point of pride that more than one friend has told me that sometimes they ask themselves, "What would Sharon do?" But I never thought of channeling my zealous pragmatism into book form until Peter Dougherty invited me to contribute to the Skills for Scholars series. I thank Peter for that invitation and for his expert guidance at the outset of this project. What Peter helped me start, Matt Rohal helped me finish. I am grateful for the acumen and engagement offered by Matt, by my five anonymous peer reviewers, and by everyone at Princeton University Press.

I like getting advice as much as I like giving it and am fortunate that a number of colleagues, friends, and family members read drafts of this book and offered detailed comments that helped improve it: Jinpa Atwood, Deborah Cohen, Matthew Fisher, Neil Goldberg, David Henkin, Yonina Hoffman, Eleanor Johnson, and Caitlin Zaloom.

I also extend my heartfelt gratitude to the colleagues who generously shared their time and wisdom in wide-ranging interviews about academic talks: Mariana Alessandri, Nicholas Dames, Daniel Immerwahr, Branden Joseph, Michèle Lamont, David Levine, Robert Mawhinney, and Rebecca Walkowitz.

When academics give and attend talks, we work together to create knowledge, in person and in real time. To deliver a talk is an act of creativity, daring, and generosity; so is listening to a talk and asking questions about it. I'll end, then, by thanking all the scholars who gave the talks this book cites, and all the audience members who responded to them, for teaching me so much about their topics and about the art of academic speaking.

A NOTE ON THE TYPE

This book has been composed in Arno, an Old-style serif typeface in the classic Venetian tradition, designed by Robert Slimbach at Adobe.

GPSR Authorized Representative: Easy Access System Europe - Mustamäe tee 50, 10621 Tallinn, Estonia, gpsr.requests@easproject.com

www.ingramcontent.com/pod-product-compliance
Lightning Source LLC
LaVergne TN
LVHW050913241026
850939LV00024BA/241

9780691249322